# The Bible Sex and You

Dr. Roy B. Blizzard is president of Bible Scholars, Inc., an Austin-based corporation dedicated to biblical research and education. He is the author of *Mishnah and the Words of Jesus, Tithing Giving and Prosperity, The Mountain of the Lord, Let Judah go up first: A study in praise, prayer, and worship,* and coauthor of *Understanding the Difficult Words of Jesus: New Insights From a Hebrew Perspective.* Visit the Bible Scholars website at www.biblescholars.org.

# The Bible Sex and You

What the Bible REALLY says about:
Marriage, Sex, Birth Control, Abortion,
Divorce, Homosexuality, Fornication,
Adultery, Masturbation
and much more!

## Roy B. Blizzard

Bible Scholars, Inc.
Austin, Texas

Copyright © 2013 by Bible Scholars, Inc.
All rights reserved.
ISBN-13: 978-1482640458

Cover design: Dan Schoenfeld

P.O. Box 204073
Austin, Texas 78720
www.biblescholars.org

Printed in the United States of America

## CONTENTS

| | |
|---|---|
| Forewords | 7 |
| Introduction by Dr. Ron Moseley | 9 |
| Note to the Reader | 13 |
| Background | 15 |
| 1 – The Role of Women | 29 |
| 2 – Modern Thought | 49 |
| 3 – Marriage | 57 |
| 4 – Orgasm | 67 |
| 5 – Judaic Thought on Human Sexuality | 73 |
| 6 – Contraception or Birth Control | 77 |
| 7 – Abortion | 81 |
| 8 – Marriage Laws and Customs | 87 |
| 9 – Homosexuality | 99 |
| 10 – Transsexualism | 109 |
| 11 – Masturbation | 115 |
| 12 – Premarital Sex | 119 |
| 13 – Conclusions and Questions | 121 |
| Appendix I | 123 |
| Appendix II | 125 |
| Endnotes | 127 |
| Bibliography | 131 |
| Glossary Of Terms | 133 |
| About the Author | 151 |

# FOREWORDS

Few honors could be attributed to an author more meaningful than to be recognized for researching and writing the truth, while knowingly looking down the barrel of contemporary religious opposition. In this present volume, Dr. Roy Blizzard has accomplished that objective. Dr. Blizzard not only researched his subject from the ancient culture and languages, but maintained academic and professional license in the field of sex and the *Bible*.

This book is well written and logical in its conclusions as the subject was understood during the biblical period. Although some religious traditionalists, who refuse to alter their views even in light of the facts, may oppose Dr. Blizzard's conclusions; few if any, will be able to contradict his findings using credible sources.

– Ron W. Moseley, Ph.D., D. Phil., Founder and President
*American Institute of Middle Eastern Studies, Sherwood, Arkansas*

I just finished reading a draft of this timely book

and offer many, many, kudos to Dr. Roy Blizzard on this outstanding accomplishment! A readable, understandable, logical book about sex! WOW! This book is a delight in making the incomprehensible understood, the confusing explained, and the "tabooed" subject of sex palatable to all!

Dr. Blizzard's direct, no-nonsense, concise approach finally brings to light what the *Bible* really says about sex. A crowning achievement, to say the very least! I am honored Dr. Blizzard elected to share his book with me prior to publication. This book will do extremely well because it is appealing to all age groups, genders, and communities, regardless of ethnicity. I look forward to working closely with Dr. Blizzard on his proposed television series, neatly covering this sensational subject matter! It certainly will captivate many millions of viewers, world-wide!

– Opher Segal, Writer/Producer
*True Dreams Imagined, LLC., Los Angeles, California*

Dr. Blizzard is one those invaluable and rare Christian scholars whose theology arises from his research into the evidence, and not the other way around. He knows the right questions to ask, and his book is not filled by the assertions of a manifesto but the answers to questions honestly asked.

– Rabbi Kerry Baker
*Everybody Needs a Rabbi – "Teaching from the heart of Judaism for all.", Austin, Texas*

# INTRODUCTION
# BY DR. RON MOSELEY

Years ago, I could only dream of the subject of sex in the *Bible* being dealt with from a historic-biblical viewpoint as opposed to religious and traditional perspectives. In accordance with that concept, I maintained a detailed research file on the subject. Sadly, unlike Dr. Blizzard, I was not courageous enough to put this subject into book form. In searching my mind for a title, numerous names surfaced including;

- *Tell Me It Ain't So!*
- *Believe It or Not*
- *I Don't Believe I Would Have Said That*
- *God Said What?*

Each title conjured thoughts of the most negative reactions from religious minded teachers and congregants alike. Just the same, it was fun imagining that one day someone might share the seemingly hidden gems about the *Bible*, sex and ancient culture.

Even the most cursory review of the subject of sex, as referenced in biblical text, would shock most modern congregants.

The primary reason for the bewilderment of contemporary readers should be laid at the feet of puritanical theologians. They have sacrificed truth, relating to ancient sexual customs, on the altar of defining lasciviousness as anything their wives refused to permit.

Major problems have arisen due to the failure of modern teachers to investigate or accept ancient sexual customs which were directly linked to biblical injunctions. Often the biblical record was not defining what was right or wrong, but correcting specific cultural moral deficiencies which no longer exist.

## CULTURE OPPOSED TO SCRIPTURE

The Apostle Paul admonished ancient believers in Corinth to honor several harmless traditions, in order to gain the trust of the pagan citizens, while reiterating that Jewish believers in Jerusalem had no such customs (*1 Corinthians* 11:16). Since each generation has dissimilar traditions, readers should interpret all biblical tenets alongside the cultural environment in which they were written.

For example, during the Greco-Roman period anyone who did not participate in emperor worship was deemed an atheist. Morality was interpreted according to an individual's success in contributing to the empire. Without understanding the vast differences in the two cultures of Corinth and Jerusalem, modern readers might logically misinterpret Paul's injunction to "flee the immorality" of Corinth, which was a popular and accepted tradition in 1st century societies (*1 Corinthians* 6:18).

Although religion and morality were the foundations of Rome, the definition of immorality was not clear. Emperor

Augustus incorporated moral laws, exiled the poet Ovid for writing an explicit sex manual and banished his daughter Julia for adultery, while requiring participants in the national games to perform naked. The ten most prominent passions of ancient Rome included binge drinking, getting naked in public gatherings, extreme violence in the Coliseum, food consumption to the point of gluttony and wealthy citizens having sex with young boys. Yet Rome considered itself moral (Ray Laurence, *Roman Passions*, Trade Press, 2010).

Sexual sins in the biblical text were addressing specific abuses in different generations, which have frustrated modern believers who are unaware that the text was describing a specific cultural tradition rather than a general biblical injunction.

## KEEP EACH COMMANDMENT IN ITS ORIGINAL CONTEXT

It never ceases to amaze scholars how religious minded teachers can twist the lucid meaning of a text referring to the consummation of sex between couples into something totally foreign to the biblical context and call it a spiritual analogy.

### THE PICTURESQUE IMAGERY OF THE HEBREW LANGUAGE

The biblical text has never been shy about describing sex in what contemporary scholars describe as erotic or sexually suggestive terms. God told Hosea the prophet to marry a whore and compared the sins of Jerusalem with graphic sexual terms, which evolved to the point that she paid her lovers (*Hosea* 1:2, 3; *Ezekiel* 16).

Sexual idioms were difficult to interpret outside their original setting; and if translated literally, would almost guarantee a misunderstanding. Picturesque Hebraic terms afford lucid descriptions of biblical terms, which otherwise might appear unclear to modern readers.

CONCLUSION

Although no one volume could address the numerous sexual incidents recorded in the biblical text, the intent of my introduction was to alert readers to the changing customs that surrounded each biblical command. The abuse of theological snooping into bedroom practices has continued to rank among the top religious offenses of church leaders. Clergy who have alluded to the possession of any authority concerning regulating the sex life of congregants should be ashamed of themselves and looked upon as pulpit "Peeping Toms."

# NOTE TO THE READER

Due to the nature of the subject matter in this manuscript, we have used various Hebrew or Greek phrases and technical terminology to help clarify and emphasize the source or original significance of certain information.

We have included an extensive glossary at the end of this work that will define most of the unfamiliar terms used in the text.

REFER TO THE GLOSSARY FREQUENTLY AS YOU READ THIS VOLUME!

We hope you will find this work helpful to gaining a healthier understanding of the Bible, sex and you.

*The most outrageous lies that can be invented will find believers if a person only tells them with all his might.*
*— Mark Twain*

# BACKGROUND

SEX! The one word that never fails to get everybody's attention: either positively or negatively. But the fact is, regardless into which category you fall, we are all sexual beings. Please indulge me a few lines of background information to set the stage for the material to follow.

I have always been interested in human history and early man. As a young man in my teens, I can remember roaming ancient Indian campsites in Missouri, Oklahoma and Kansas, collecting Indian artifacts of one kind or another. Today, I still have a large collection of artifacts that I have gathered over the years.

While studying at Oklahoma Military Academy, in addition to military I included a major in science thinking that one day I may teach science. After leaving the Military Academy, I enrolled at Phillips University in Enid, Oklahoma. Because I was a sophomore when I enrolled, I had to take Greek and several courses in religion. One of the courses was Pastoral Counseling along with a lot of

Philosophy and Psychology. While still a student at Phillips and before I graduated, I was offered a little preaching point where I spoke every Sunday on a regular basis until graduation. After graduation, I was offered another congregation and spent a number of years pastoring at Independent Christian churches until 1960 when I was offered a congregation in Lovington, New Mexico.

In 1964, I had the opportunity to go back to school at Eastern New Mexico University and work on a Master's Degree in Anthropology/Archaeology and Religion. In the religion courses, I was exposed to much new information. The head of the program came from a Jewish background and his father had been a rabbi. On the other hand, I had the opportunity to work with the head of the Department of Anthropology/Archaeology and took courses until finally it was only the professor and me in the class. At the same time, I had the opportunity to continue with field work, excavating at several sites dating back as early as the Paleolithic period.

After graduation, I had the good fortune to be invited to study archaeology at the Hebrew University in Jerusalem! During the summer of 1966, I studied archaeology at the Hebrew University in Jerusalem. In addition to the classroom work, we traveled extensively on the weekends, visiting many of the important archaeological sites. One of the sites we visited was one of the earliest early-man sites in the world: the Carmel Caves and the immediate area along the Carmel range where over 200 skeletons of *Homo (H.) sapien sapiens* (see photos) have been found along with skeletons or partial skeletons from earlier periods. Later, I took the opportunity to visit the area of the Border Cave in the Natal Province in South Africa where skeletons of *H. sapien sapiens*, dating as early as 70-80,000 years before they were ever imagined to have appeared on the evolutionary scale of development, were found in the 1960's.

*The Carmel Caves in Israel where more than 200 early-man skeletons were found.*

*The Carmel Caves are one of the earliest archaeological sites in the world where Homo sapien sapiens were discovered.*

*Dr. Blizzard lecturing to students at the Carmel Caves at the site where some of the skeletons were found.*

*Skeleton found at the Carmel Caves.*

It was during my study in Israel that I came to the realization that most of what I had learned in my courses in religion in the United States was outdated or in error. As a result, I decided to go back to school at the University of Texas at Austin where I finished another Master's Degree in the general field of Hebrew studies and, finally, my Ph.D. in the same field. I continued studying in Israel, traveling there anywhere from 3-5 times a year, and continuing with my study and excavating at different archaeological sites including the Temple Mount in Jerusalem.

During my time pastoring churches in Oklahoma and New Mexico, an interesting thing had happened. Since I had a background in psychology and counseling, people started gravitating toward me for counseling. Although I tried my best, I never really felt qualified in the field. Again, an interesting thing happened. Most of the problems people were bringing to me centered on one or two issues: either sex or money – or a combination of the two.

As a result of my studies in Israel, I knew there was a considerable difference between the Christian sex ethic and the Jewish sex ethic. So, I went back to school and studied human sexuality. In the 1980's I was conferred the title of "Certified Sex Educator" by the American Association of Sex

Educators, Counselors and Therapists and then in the early 90's as a Diplomate of the American Board of Sexology. I have maintained in the ensuing years a small private practice in the field and over the years have seen the need for competent sex education and therapy to increase considerably.

Recently – and read this paragraph carefully – there have been several new books that have appeared in the marketplace written by religionists on the subject of sex. In many cases, they were written by religious leaders who were largely uneducated and uncredentialed in either the field of human sexuality or biblical studies. In most instances, the author attempted to inform the general public about what is and what is not acceptable insofar as what the *Bible* has to say on the subject of sex. They were written only from a Christian perspective and reflect simply the author's own peculiar or particular view on the subject. Because it was written from a Christian perspective exclusively, much of the information was, simply stated, wrong! Not just wrong, but destructive because the information, if followed, could lead the individual or couple involved into error, misinformation and misunderstanding.

I certainly believe their intentions were good. They were trying to instruct their constituency on the biblical position relating to sex and marriage. But, there was one basic problem: in order to understand what the biblical position is on any subject and, particularly on the subject of sex, one has to do it from a Hebrew perspective.

One tends to overlook the fact that the *Bible* in its entirety is a Hebrew document. To learn what the biblical position is on this subject, one has to examine it from a Hebrew point of view. To do that, we have to look at it over a period of over 3,000 years and from a historical and cultural perspective. Two thousand years ago, the perspective on a given subject may have been one thing. During the first century of the present era it may have been something else again. During the Middle Ages it may have been something quite different.

Today, our perspective on sex is something essentially rational and objective. Perhaps the biggest problem of all is that one has about 1700 years of Christian thought on the subject to try to overcome – Christian thought that goes all the way back to the Stoics and Cynics of Greek philosophy and incorporates many of their ideas into the theology of the Church. Things could only go from bad to worse!

## LOOKING AT THE ARTIFACTS

As a result of recent archaeological finds throughout Africa and the Middle East, the whole of anthropology has been thrown into a complete state of chaos relative to our understanding of human development, especially compared to what we were taught in the 40's and 50's, i.e., that man was the end product of a long line of evolutionary development from Dryopithecus and Ramapithecus, Australopithecus, Neanderthal, Mousterian, and, finally – Shazam! *Homo sapien sapiens*!

It now seems evident that our ancestry goes back perhaps 4-5 million years. Recently the artistic representation of one of our early ancestors, dating from perhaps 4 million years ago, Ardipithecus Ramidus, was published. The last few decades have seen astonishing discoveries about human origins that add greatly to our understanding of what it means to be human. The Smithsonian Museum of Natural History has an exceptionally informative Web site on the subject that offers the best and most up to date information on the subject of what it means to be human. You may access all the information by simply typing "human origin" into your search engine. As you will soon see from the material presented, we know much today about our ancestral lineage and man's development toward humankind and yet we know little or nothing about human sexuality.

We know one thing at least: that from a very early period of time, our early ancestors were certainly interested in sex! This interest is further illustrated by the many Venus figurines from many widely separated geographical areas, as well as the vast separation in time. Visit Don's Maps at www.donsmaps.com/venus.html to view illustrations of the many and varied Venus figurines.

In the various archaeological excavations and from the many and varied artifacts and monumental remains, we know much about how they lived. Yet, for thousands upon thousands of years, we know little or nothing about their sexuality.

One thing we do know is that about 10,000 years ago humankind took a giant step forward from the hunter/fisher to the farmer/gatherer and began to settle into an established community atmosphere. An example of one of these communities is Jericho, the oldest continuously occupied site in the world, dating back into the pre-pottery Neolithic period, perhaps as early as 10,000 years ago.

We know a lot from our excavations at such sites as to how they lived, what they ate, the types of crops they grew, the animals they raised and domesticated, the animals they hunted and how they buried their dead. We know a lot. And, still we know little or nothing about their sex lives.

Then, about 5,500 years ago, man takes another giant step forward. Why? What happened? How did it happen? We can only guess. But, it happened all over the Middle East and all the way down into Egypt: the invention of writing – in Mesopotamia, Sumerian, Acadian, Babylonian, Old Persian, Cuneiform and, of course, the South and West Egyptian hieroglyphics.

About 12-1500 BCE, the invention of the alphabet both simplified and greatly advanced writing. Suddenly, instead of having to use 3,000 or more characters to communicate an idea, it could now be greatly simplified with an alphabet of only 22 to 26 different characters. Ugaritic, Aramaic, Canaanite, Hebrew, Edomite, Ethiopic and many other written languages allowed man to communicate with each other from north and east in Mesopotamia all the way down into Egypt. We were able to learn something about man – not only how he lived, but what he thought. Now we began to learn something about what he thought about sex without having to conjecture or guess.

In our archaeological excavations of the ancient civilizations throughout Mesopotamia all the way down into Egypt we found, in many of the cities that were excavated, the royal archives with thousands of documents in the various languages, many of which have now been translated. From these documents, we learned much about every aspect of the life and culture of the inhabitants of these ancient cities. Interestingly enough, we find from some of the oldest of the documents that they were just as interested in the subject of sex, then, as man is now. Just as the *Song of Solomon* in the biblical text has obvious erotic implication, so, too, do some of the oldest of these documents contain obviously erotic implications. One such document from Sumeria is entitled *Lettuce is my Hair*.

Lettuce was actually considered an aphrodisiac in the ancient near east because when this particular type of lettuce goes to seed it shoots up tall and releases a milky white sap. Another such song is called *The Honeyman*, which is a love song to a king. The translation is as follows:

> He has *sprouted*, he has *burgeoned*, he is lettuce planted by the water,
> My well-stocked garden of the...plain, my favored of the womb,
> My grain luxuriant in its furrow – he is lettuce *planted by* the water,

> My apple tree which bears fruit up to (its) top – he is lettuce *planted by* the water.
> The "honey-man," the "honey-man" sweetens me ever,
> My lord, the "honey-man" of the gods, my favored of the *womb*,
> Whose hand is honey, whose foot is honey, sweetens me ever.
> Whose limbs are honey sweet, sweetens me ever.
> My sweetener of the...navel, (my favoured of the *womb*),
> My...of the fair thighs, he is lettuce (*planted by* the water).
> It is a *balbale* (poem) of Inanna.[1]

Our oldest written records come from the civilization of Sumer. Some of these documents date back as far as 3100 BCE and, from the libraries excavated throughout Mesopotamia, we are able to ascertain that a flourishing literature developed. This literature contains a large collection of erotic poems, love songs, expressions of love between a man and a woman and poems that suggest a very close relationship between the poems of ancient Sumer and the biblical *Song of Solomon*.

## LOVE POETRY OF EGYPT AND MESOPOTAMIA

The story unraveled with the young man referring to the girl as sister and bride, which were ancient terms of endearment denoting the couple's closeness and intention to marry. The girl was no more his bride at that point of the narrative than she was his sister (Ariel Bloch, *The Song of Songs*, University Press Berkeley, 1998). Although the metaphors and similes are not easily understood by modern readers, in ancient love poetry of Egypt and Mesopotamia it was common to refer to the girl as a garden with similar literary genres calling the male a brother and king, the woman as a garden and the field as the location of the couple's sexual exploits.

Although there are numerous uncertainties about the identity of the characters, there remained little doubt that the central theme related to sexual love. The *Song of Solomon* was almost completely composed of the woman's dream of what true love would involve as she described to her friends the exaggerated attributes of her lover (2:15-17; 5:10-16; 8:12).

The ultimate theme appears to have been in accordance with the original value, which God placed on true love and the beauty of the way of a man with a woman (*Genesis* 1:27-28; *Proverbs* 30:18,19).

## LATER REVISIONS OF THE SONG OF SOLOMON

Several modern translations have repeated the practice of the Greek manuscripts, such as the *Sinaiticus* from 400 CE, which added the terms "bride" and "bridegroom" in an effort to indicate that the original setting was a marriage ceremony (*Anchor Bible Commentary*). Much controversy has arisen, due to little evidence supporting any marriage other than the mention of the majestic wedding procession of Solomon on his wedding day (3:11). Although the *Song of Solomon* was not written as an allegory, the traditional method of interpretation has been to allegorize the sexual tone and replace the original intention with an allusion to the love between God and His people. While there are numerous biblical passages, which illustrated the love between God and Israel in terms of lovers, each text explicitly identified the relationship as God and Israel (*Hosea* 2:4-23; *Isaiah* 62:4, 5). There was no such identification in the *Song of Solomon* and the explicit sexual language was obviously between a man and woman. After the middle of the 20th century, modern scholarship has shifted to the recognition that the literal interpretation was directed at human love (*Anchor Bible Commentary*, Volume 6).

Note several erotic phrases found in the pages of the *Song of Solomon*:

- "He shall lie all night betwixt my breasts" (1:13).
- "His left hand is under my head and his right hand doth embrace me" (2:6, 7).
- "Stir not up, nor awake my love, till he please" (3:5).
- "Your two breasts are like two fawns, like twin fawns of a gazelle that browse among the lilies" (4:5).
- "Let my lover come into his garden and taste its delicious fruits" (4:16).
- She and her lover meet secretly in the countryside at night and part at daybreak, which to some has indicated a pre-marital episode.
- "Come...blow upon my garden that the spices thereof may flow out. Let my beloved come into his garden, and eat his pleasant fruits" (4:16).
- "We have a little sister, and she hath no breasts...but my breasts are like towers" (8:8-10).
- "I found him whom my soul loveth: I held him, and would not let him go, until I had brought him into my mother's house and into the chamber of her that conceived me" (3:4).
- "Thy lips, O my spouse, drop as the honeycomb: honey and milk are under thy tongue; and the smell of thy garments is like the smell of Lebanon" (4:11).
- "The joints of thy thighs are like jewels" (7:1).
- "Thy navel is like a round goblet, which wanteth not liquor: thy belly is like an heap of wheat set about with lilies" (7:2).
- "Thy breasts to clusters of grapes" (7:7).
- "Come, my beloved, let us go forth into the field...Let us get up early to the vineyards...there will I give thee my loves" (7:12).
- "I would cause thee to drink of spiced wine of the juice of my pomegranate" (8:2).

*(The above information relating to the Song of Solomon was contributed by Dr. Ron Moseley)*

With the onset of civilization and the voluminous amount of written literature from these ancient civilizations, it is now a relatively easy task to re-create the societies of the ancient world that extended from Mesopotamia south and west all the way to Egypt. I think it is safe to say that a climate was created in which man assumed the dominant role in society and woman focused her energies on husband and the home.

From the earliest of times of *H. sapien sapiens*' existence, our knowledge of his personal life is based largely on speculation arising from debris found in living quarters, caves, in mounds; from tools and artifacts of various sizes and shapes and from skeletal remains. From these artifacts, we assume that the male went out hunting while the females stayed behind to care for the children. It appears, from skeletal remains, that women outnumbered men by perhaps as many as two to one. However, a man could expect to outlive the woman by as many as 8-10 years. Life expectancy was low. Only two out of ten people lived to the age of 30. The average woman probably had only 15 years or so between puberty and death. Even today, in many places around the world, the infant mortality rate is as high as 45-50 percent. Just to maintain a zero-population growth, prehistoric woman would have had to have raised four children.

Polygamy seems to have been the norm. Paleolithic woman spent most of her time either pregnant or nursing; at least, we so conclude from the various surviving Venus figurines that have been discovered. Most are explicitly sexual, suggesting either a fertility cult or at least more than a passive interest in sex.

Female figurines from prehistoric times have been found in countries as widely diverse as Germany, Russia, and Israel, undoubtedly, representing the wide spread existence of fertility cults. These female figurines, often labeled Venuses, may reflect a fertility cult or may be nothing more than prehistoric pin-up girls.

With the onset of civilization, a climate was created in which man assumed the dominant role in society and woman focused her energies on husband and the home. However, in the history of ancient Greece and Rome there were many talented and exceptional women mentioned; such as, Sappho (625-570 BCE) and Aspasia (470-400 BCE) who was Milesian and famous for her involvement with Athenian statesman Pericles.

Sappho was born into an aristocratic family and, although little is known for certain about her life, she is included in the list of nine lyric poets. The bulk of her poetry has been lost but her immense reputation has endured. Very little is known about Aspasia, although she spent most of her adult life in Athens. Ancient writers reported that she was a brothel keeper and the mistress to Pericles. The *hetaerae* were professional high-class entertainers as well as courtesans. They differed from most Athenian women by being educated and were, perhaps, the nearest thing to a liberated woman in ancient times.

## CHAPTER 1
# THE ROLE OF WOMEN

With the advent of writing, civilization took another giant leap forward. However, in this new environment, the woman was considered inferior. There were very few ways in which a woman could support herself outside the home. A woman was essentially either a wife or a slave.

In order to escape the tyranny of the home, some women became hairdressers, singers, or fortune-tellers, while others devoted themselves to the service of the gods. The role of harlot carried no stigma in ancient times. Temples were generally staffed by cult prostitutes, both male and female, whose earnings accounted for a substantial part of the temple income. The Greek historian, Herodotus, was awed by the number of temple prostitutes. In *The Histories*, he reports:

> Every woman who is a native of the country must once in her life go and sit in the temple and there

give herself to a strange man. She is not allowed to go home until the man has thrown a silver coin into her lap and taken her outside to lie with her. The woman has no privilege of choice. She must go with the first man who throws her the money. When she has lain with him, her duty to the goddess is discharged and she may go home. Handsome women soon manage to get home again but the ugly ones stay a long time before they can fulfill the condition which the law demands, some of them indeed as much as 3-4 years.[2]

Sacred prostitutes were classified into groups although their exact function is unknown. There were the *Harmitu* and the *Qadishtu*. *Harmitu* is related to the word *harem*; *Qadishtu*, to the word *holy* or *sacred*. *Ishtaritu* served the goddess Ishtar. High-ranking prostitutes were part of the temple, while others plied their trade in the streets and public places.

The prostitute was not to cover or veil her head in public. In the ancient world, sex was of minor import. The wealthy and the rich had numerous foreign slave girls, while streets and temples were well supplied with different classes of prostitutes. Casual sex was often supplied by traveling dancers and musicians who considered it a secondary trade.

By the time of ancient Greece and Rome, the classical authors had created a vivid depiction that has given us *androgyny, aphrodisiac, eroticism, hermaphroditicism, homosexual, narcissism, nymphomania, pederasty, satyriasis zoophilia* – all Greek in origin and all relating to activities found in classical authorship.

From the 6th to the early 4th century BCE, pederasty flourished throughout Greece although the Greeks staunchly maintained that it was a branch of higher education. Many of the Roman authors, such as Horace and Martial, were pederasts or homosexuals.

Strato of Lampsacus (d 270 BCE), who devoted himself to the philosophy of Aristotle: "The bloom of a 12-year-old boy is desirable, but at 13 he is much more delightful, sweeter still is the flower of love that blossoms at 14, his charm increases at 15 and 16 is the divine age."

In ancient Greece, women were subject to the absolute authority of their male next-of-kin. They had no more political or legal rights than slaves and received no formal education. They spent most of their time in the women's quarters at home and seldom went out of doors or even dined with their husband. A wife could obtain a divorce only on the grounds of extreme provocation – which did not include pederasty or adultery. To the ancient Greeks, a woman was *gyne*, literally a bearer of children. Domestic harmony was basically unknown.

These Greeks considered the best age for a man to marry was 30. And 16 for the girl, although they considered that it was better to buy than to marry her. Usually the girl was 13 or 14 and was expected to have intercourse with her husband at least three times a month until she became pregnant.

Because of the Greek male's view of woman, there would certainly have been an excess of unmarried women had it not been for the high male mortality rate in the frequent wars. To offset what would have been a grave imbalance, the Greeks resorted to infanticide for population control.

Large families were generally uncommon. Neglected wives frequently resorted to homosexuality. One prosperous business venture was the manufacture of the olisbos, which we know today as dildos. These were used not only by straight women but by women homosexuals known as tribads. Tribadism was common throughout the Greek world, the Island of Lesbos being the heartland.

During the later part of the 4th century BCE and on into the 3rd, men of Athens began to show more interest in women – although not necessarily to their wives. As a result of the conquests of Alexander the Great, men had more time and money to spend and frequently did so on hetairai and concubines. Prostitutes too flourished so that the temple of Aphrodite at Corinth boasted more than 1,000 cult prostitutes dedicated to the service of the goddess.

Roman women faced much the same conditions as the women in Greece. Chastity was not a major virtue! Rather, it had become a virtue scarcely seen in Rome since the Golden Age (the time of Augustus 63 BCE to 14 CE). The lot of the Roman woman was dire. She could be killed on the spot if caught in adultery and could be divorced if she drank more than a minimum amount of wine, For such drinking indicated, in their culture, moral ineptitude and sexual laxity. Infertility provided grounds for divorce as well.

Wives and children were property, although in Rome the woman was expected to play a more active role in maintaining home and family. But upper-class women enjoyed a liberty rare in the ancient world. For they were allowed to do basically as they liked: beautifying themselves; spending money; and, as one philosopher put it, mastering the art of laboriously doing nothing.

There can be little doubt of the educational accomplishment of many women in ancient Greece and Rome. Mainly, women were educated at home except for music and dance lessons. Often they were educated by their husbands, brothers or fathers and some Greek and Roman women were obviously very well educated. Cult prostitutes had special schools where they learned entertaining, conversation and rhetoric. Slaves, on the other hand, were not educated. The customary branches of education were four in number: 1 - reading and writing, 2 - gymnastic exercises, 3 - music and 4 - drawing. Girls were trained for marriage while boys were educated to become warriors. In Sparta, the education of girls took place in the sanctuaries of Artemis, the goddess of maidenhood. Of course, a major focus of girls' education was their training for motherhood.[3]

## WOMEN IN ANCIENT GREECE AND ROME

Religion offered women escape from boredom. Many of Rome's deities took on attributes of the Greek gods. The Roman god Liber, for example, took on attributes of the Greek god Priapus, represented by a phallic symbol and Dionysus, god of vineyards, became Bacchus, god of drink and drunkenness. Venus merged with Aphrodite and became patron of harlots frequenting the *Circus Maximus* or the camp of the Praetorian Guard. Cybele was known as the Great Goddess. Mithras, Isis, and Serapis followed.

In spite of the excitement of festivals and celebrations such as the Bacchanalia, by the beginning of the 2$^{nd}$ century CE the Roman family was beginning to fall apart. Husbands divorced their wives because of their wrinkles or because they were immoral. Women divorced their husbands because they were bored.

One Roman official remarked sardonically: "If it were possible to live without wives, we should all save ourselves the trouble. But since nature has decreed that we can neither live with them in peace nor without them at all, we should act with future benefits rather than present comfort in mind."

When Cicero divorced his wife, Terentia, he was asked whether he would marry again. He replied: "Certainly not! I could not cope with philosophy and a wife at the same time." It appears that Roman women and Roman men were equally difficult to live with.

The history of Greece and Rome is replete with names of strong-minded women; such as Sappho and Aspasia. They tended to run wild. The "taming" of a girl is expressed in a number of myths that all circle around her resistance to "domestication." In an essentially masculine society, the question arises: "How did they get away with it?" Perhaps sexual mischief kept them out of the political arena. But even more likely, perhaps the Roman husband did not much care what his wife did so long as she just left him alone.

## INFANTICIDE AS BIRTH CONTROL

There was, however, one crucial problem. There were not enough women to go around. The law of Romulus had urged parents to raise all male children but only the first-born girl. In most cities there were places specifically set aside for the abandonment of unwanted infants, usually females, but also males who were deformed or illegitimate. Another problem was infant mortality. Relatively few survived infancy. Up until the 4th century, infanticide was a major method of population control all through the Roman Empire. It continued in Europe until the 17th century.

Those who chose to marry usually wanted, at most, only two or three children. Moreover, there was plenty of contraceptive information available by now. And there was always abstinence. Failing that, however, men generally relied on *coitus interruptus* while women relied on the olive oil method. In the 4th century BCE, Aristotle gave advice on how to prevent pregnancy. He advised women to use olive oil, lead ointment, or frankincense oil as a spermicide. His intentions were good, but his methods flawed. About 200 CE, the Greek gynecologist, Soranus of Ephesus, suggested smearing olive oil, pomegranate pulp, or ginger around the vagina to kill sperm.

Usually prostitutes insisted on anal intercourse. There are indications that the Romans may have invented condoms from goat bladders. But it is quite possible, as we shall see, that they may not have needed them.

Only recently have we learned that upper-class Romans suffered from chronic lead poisoning, causing sterility in men and miscarriages or stillbirths in women. Romans absorbed lead from water that ran through lead pipes into their homes and so into their baths. They also drank from lead cups and ate from lead cooking pots. In addition, they habitually sweetened their foods with grape syrup that had been boiled in lead pots. Yet if Roman men escaped sterility from lead poisoning, they were still in danger of impotence from alcoholism. And that was not all.

Every time a man went to the bath – and most men went every day – he further endangered his potency. That is, his power to produce offspring. For the hot bath inhibited sperm production through the high temperature of the caldarium.

By the end of the 1st century BCE, the Romans were aware of the falling birthrate. Certain laws were enacted to encourage couples to multiply. Unfortunately, these laws came too late. The lack of manpower marked the downfall of Rome.

## THE RISE OF MESSIANISM

By the beginning of the 1st century CE, the world was ruled by Rome. From England to Africa, from Syria to Spain, one in every four people on earth lived and died under Roman law. In the Roman outpost of Judea, during the reign of the Emperor Tiberius, a Jewish religious leader from Galilee gave birth to a new movement within Judaism that would turn the Empire upside down and ultimately reshape the whole world.

At its inception, this new movement operated strictly within the framework of historical Judaism with all its laws and customs. It was a Jewish movement and, as such, operated within the religious framework in which Judaism had operated since its return from Babylon in 538 BCE – with one notable exception.

As a result of the preaching of Jesus and those who came after him, it became a missionary movement. The preaching of Yahweh (*YHWH*) as the one and only God, not just of Jews but of all peoples, was exported throughout the Roman world. As the movement moved to the West, it ran headlong into Greek and Roman philosophy.

It is here in the Greek/Roman world that Judaism, with its unique ethic of the legitimacy of sexual pleasure, runs headlong into the philosophy that would ultimately serve as the foundation upon which the Christian sex ethic of the $4^{th}$ and $5^{th}$ centuries – and that survives today – would be built. Stoicism was the foremost philosophy among the elite in the Hellenistic world and the world of the Roman Empire. So much so that nearly all the successors of Alexander the Great professed themselves Stoics.

Stoicism was founded in Athens by Zeno of Citium in the early $3^{rd}$ century BCE. The basic teaching of the Stoic was fortitude and self-control. The Stoic was to be free of passion, reliant only upon reason; and so indifferent to pleasure, pain, and the vicissitudes of fortune. Stoicism held that virtue is the highest good, and that virtue is based on wisdom. Wisdom, in turn, is based upon harmony with divine Reason. Stoicism shared much in common with Cynicism. The story of Cynicism traditionally begins with Antisthenes (c 445-365 BCE) Antisthenes was a contemporary of Plato and a student of Socrates.

Cynicism held the goal of life to be happiness. Happiness depends on being self- sufficient. One must free himself from the influences of wealth, fame, power, and the like. The Cynic, then, is ascetic – requiring only the basic necessities of life. Virtue is the only good, its essence residing in self-control and independence.

## EARLY CHRISTIANITY

Unfortunately, many of the practices of Cynicism and Stoicism – and especially that of asceticism and later on celibacy – were adopted by the early Christians. As a result, asceticism and self-denial, seclusion and austerity, celibacy and monasticism are characteristics of Catholicism to this very day. It is of the utmost importance to note that such other-worldliness, quite aside from the vital issue of sexual pleasure, is alien to Judaism!

Mosheh ben Maimon, called Moses Maimonides and

also known as RaMBaM, (1135-1204) was a preeminent medieval Jewish philosopher and one of the most prolific and followed Torah scholars and physicians of the Middle Ages. He expressed the typical view of the Jew of his day: "One might say: 'inasmuch as jealousy, passion, love of honor may bring about man's downfall, I will, therefore, remove myself to the other extreme. I will refrain from meat and wine, marriage or a pleasant home or attractive garments...this is an evil way and forbidden. He who follows these practices is a sinner.'"

In Judaism, the renunciation of the pleasures of this world is characteristically regarded as sinful ingratitude to the Creator. One Talmudic sage even declared: "Man will have to render an account to God for all the good things which his eyes beheld but which he refused to enjoy." Of the good things, sex had a status of its own.

Early Christianity, as it moved to the West and so off Jewish soil, departed from Judaism in general and in particular. In general, it departed by its attitude toward worldly pleasures at large. In particular, it departed by its attitude toward sex. Abstinence became the criterion of spiritual excellence. The Christian was to employ every available means: fasting, solitude, prayer, and the like. As D. S. Bailey points out: "The decisive test was that of sexual continence. The Church fathers treat continence as the 'first fruit of faith' and significantly regard it as 'a new and distinctively Christian virtue.'"[4]

Accordingly, coitus was singled out for special contempt by the early Church fathers: mainly Tertullian, Arnobius, and Jerome. But it remained for Augustine to designate it as the vehicle of original sin.

It is important to note in this connection that in times of calamity when asceticism did invade the Jewish community, sexual abstemiousness was still not encouraged. Professor Gershom Scholem, in *Major Trends in Jewish Mysticism*, reports:

> There is one important aspect in which medieval Hasidism differed sharply from its Christian contemporaries. It does not enjoin sexual asceticism. On the contrary, the greatest importance is assigned in the Sefer Hasidim or the Book of the Righteous to the establishment and maintenance of a reasonable marital life. Nowhere is penitence extended to sexual abstinence in marital relations. At no time was sexual asceticism accorded the dignity of a religious value and the mystics make no exception.[5]

It was Augustine (355-430 CE), over 300 years after the establishment of the movement of Jesus, who fostered a new system of religious thought. Augustine was Bishop of Hippo in Africa and he is the architect of a system of thought that, together with the complement of Thomas Aquinas in the 13th century, formed the twin pillars of the sexual stance of the Classical Church.

Reading back from *Genesis* 3:7, Augustine reasoned that, before the fall, sexual activity in the Garden had been fully under control, but that afterward, it became only partially so. Augustine declared that Adam and Eve then became conscious within themselves of a new and destructive impulse – lust – generated by their rebellion. Their awareness of their nakedness was an awareness of the disobedience of their genitals; no longer innocent, no longer amenable to the will of God. Shame followed and they could not bear to look upon the consequences of their sin. Their genitals had to be concealed lest they betray the truth of the Fall. And the consequences of this sin would be transmitted through the sexual act from one generation to the next. Lust, indeed, would continually reveal itself as the passion of passions, the sin of sins. For it, above all human impulses, turns one away from reason. It can be satisfied only in an orgasm which engulfs the rational faculties in violent sexual excitement.

## THE DOCTRINE OF ORIGINAL SIN

This line of thought led Augustine to equate the sex act with Original Sin so that "every child," Augustine asserted, "can be said literally to have been conceived in the sin of its parents." For Augustine, *Psalm* 51:7 supplies the primary support of teaching that original sin is both sexually defined and hereditarily transmitted.

> Behold, I was brought forth in inequity and in sin did my mother conceive me.

By contrast, Jewish sources beg to differ on *Psalm* 51:7. None considers it as asserting the sinfulness of conception or the inherited nature of sin, as Rabbi Moses Alsheik (16th century), a pupil of Rabbi Joseph Karo, declared: David is referring to the sin of illegitimate sex of his earlier ancestors who were guilty of it.[6] Namely, the daughter of Lot whose union with her inebriated father gave birth to Moab from whence came Ruth; and Boaz, whose union with Ruth (because she was from Moab) was not entirely proper. Rabbi David Altschul (17th century) of Galicia declared: the act by which I was born resembles the act of which I am guilty. Legitimate sexual activity simply cannot be called evil. Most certainly whatever was the sin of Adam and Eve, it cannot be transmitted to their descendants[7]

Ahhh...Sin! There is the rub. Just exactly what is sin? We hear it from the pulpits, from every denomination, but does anybody ever define it? Does anybody tell us just exactly what is or what is not a sin?

In Hebrew, there are 20 different words that denote sin. The ancient Hebrews had more concepts expressing various nuances of sin than exists in western thought or theology. The basic word used in the *Bible* 459 times is *chet*. It corresponds to the modern idea of *offense* rather than to that of "sin," which is a theological concept. It can be seen as a failure to fulfill one's obligation in relation to another.

Another word, *pesha*, used 136 times, is considered to be a *breach*; such as, the *breach* of a covenant. The noun avon is found 229 times and designates *crookedness*, or to be *bent*. The sinner is one who has failed in his relation to God insofar as he has not fulfilled his obligation. He has fallen short or he has missed the mark.

In Hebrew, there are two categories of sin. The first category is the Willful Sin in which one willfully ignores or transgresses God's specific commandment. An example of a Willful Sin would be the stories of Cain (*Genesis* 4), Nadab and Abihu (*Leviticus* 10: 1-2) in the *Old Testament* and in the *New Testament*, Ananias and Sapphira (*Acts* 5). When someone commits a Willful Sin, he is simply cut off. There are no provisions made for his atonement. The second category can be defined as the "Missing of the Mark." In addition, there can be sins of omission and sins of commission. For these sins, repentance brings about forgiveness.

Sin, in Hebrew/Jewish thought, is caused by the evil inclination (*Yetzer Ha-Ra*), i.e., the force in man which drives him to gratify his instincts and ambition. Although it is called the evil inclination because it often leads man to wrongdoing, yet it is essential to life in that it provides life with its driving force. It is important to note that although man is bound to sin because of the *Yetzer Ha-Ra*, this view is far removed from the Christian doctrine of original sin. In the *Talmud*, *Kiddushin* 30b,

> God says: My children! I created the evil inclination, but I created the Torah as its antidote; if you occupy yourselves with the Torah, you will not be delivered into the inclination's hand.

I think it is important to note the difference between the concepts of sin in Hebrew thought as opposed to that in Christianity.

In fundamental Christian thought, sin is going to send you straight to hell. In Hebrew thought, the idea would be generally speaking, repent, try harder and don't do it again.

As long as we are on the subject, we might as well discuss a related subject which has to do with eternal punishment and/or the hereafter. In Hebrew, it is simply known as *Olam Haba* or "the world to come" and it is rarely discussed. Whereas, Christianity spends an inordinate amount of time discussing the hereafter, heaven and hell and what they are going to be like.

In the *Mishnah*, *Order Moed*, *Tractate Chagigah* or "festivals," Chapter 2, *Mishnah* 1, it says:

> Whoever puts his mind to these four matters it would be better for him had he not come into the world: What is above. What is below. What is in the future. And what is in the past. For any discussion on these four subjects is nothing more than useless speculation and idle prognostication and serves no worthwhile academic or philosophical purpose but only causes a falling away from true moral teaching.

Let us note once again that Augustine epitomized the general attitude among the Early Church Fathers that the sex act was fundamentally disgusting. He admitted that he had constantly prayed to God to give him chastity – only not yet. Others among the Early Church Fathers – Tertullian and Jerome, for examples, had led full and active sex lives before converting to celibacy. Arnobius called the act filthy and degrading, Methodius called it unseemly, Tertullian called it shameful, and Jerome called it unclean, while Ambrose called it defilement. There was a consensus that God should have thought of a better way of dealing with procreation.

Lust and sex were integral to the doctrine of Original Sin. Every act of coitus was necessarily evil and every child was born into sin. Accordingly, celibacy was to be the badge of moral authority. In 386 CE, Pope Siricius, in what seems to have been the first authentic papal decree, had attempted to prohibit presbyters and deacons from having intercourse with their wives. The response was unanimous. It had no effect.

Before we continue, I want to add a note on the subject of lust. It happens to be one of the major issues with which I have had to deal. This subject bothers many more men than women, but regrettably, many men are troubled unduly by what they feel to be the excess burden of lust. Unfortunately, few actually know what lust means from a biblical perspective.

In Hebrew, lust is the word *hamad*. *Hamad* in a bad sense means inordinate, ungoverned, selfish desire; desire of an idolatrous tendency; desire that motivates the individual to possess the thing desired at any cost.[8] There is nothing wrong with looking, thinking, and/or fantasizing. We all have sexual thoughts and sexual fantasies – and they are normal. Only two classes of people do not have sexual thoughts or fantasies. The first class is known as liars. The second class we will call, sadly, dead! Everyone else has sexual thoughts and/or fantasies and there is nothing wrong with them! They are quite normal. It is only when the thoughts or fantasies motivate one to wrong actions that they become destructive.

A good biblical example would be King David. He looked out of his palace and saw a beautiful woman, Bathsheba, taking a bath. He probably thought, "That is a lovely woman. She has a great body!" He might even have thought, "I wonder what it would be like to possess her." All of that was quite normal. When he actually took her for his wife and sent her husband, Uriah, up to the front line in battle, he moved from a normal human response into an offense.

It is perfectly normal for a person to have sexual thoughts and/or fantasies. The best way to deal with these rather than letting them become an undue burden is to sit down and discuss them with your mate or partner and maybe there will be a way in which you can fulfill these fantasies together. Do not let them become an undue burden!

## PLEASURE AND THE LAW OF MARRIAGE

Pope Gregory I (540-604) declared that the evil element in coitus is to be found not in the act itself nor in the concupiscence or lust that impels it, but in the peculiar sensual pleasure accompanying it. Even lawful intercourse is always sinful and more so when the dominant motive of the couple is not procreation. For Gregory, then, coital evil lies not in the inordinate impulse of concupiscence but in acquiescence of the will and the enjoyment thereof.

Gregory's view was somewhat modified by Thomas Aquinas (1224-1274) some six centuries later when the medieval Scholastics revealed, in a lesser degree, the same essential antipathy to carnal intercourse displayed in the literature of the early Church. They, too, found the coital act a source of theological shame. Aquinas located the seat of coital evil not in the act itself nor even in the venereal pleasure – but in what he regarded as the inevitable irrationality of the act. As Augustine, influenced by Platonic dualism, had viewed with suspicion anything deflecting from contemplation of the eternal; so Aquinas, equally inspired by Aristotle's doctrine of the Golden Mean, found an element of evil in whatever disturbed the exercise of reason.[9]

The final decision of the Scholastics was that coital pleasure was not sinful as such but could not be engaged in without sin. Within marriage, the sin was always venial, or pardonable. Outside of marriage the sin was mortal.

Pope Gregory defined original sin with regard to the pleasure accompanying the sex act. In so doing he "out-Augustined" Augustine! In practice, he became the most extreme voice in the matter of sexual pleasure. "Not only is pleasure an unlawful purpose in intercourse," he declared in his pastoral rules, "but if any pleasure is mixed with it, the married have transgressed the law of marriage and they have befouled their intercourse thereby."

This doctrine was reiterated by Hugh of Pisa (d. 1210), a canon lawyer: "coitus can never be without sin, for it always occurs and is exercised with a certain pleasure." From the 12th-15th century era, even the milder Catholic theologians called *brutish* the permitting of intercourse for mere pleasure. Amazingly, this position remained a basic law of the Church until 1917. Much earlier, Pope Innocent III (1161-1216) had asserted that the sex act was so shameful as to be inherently wicked!

Peter Lombard (c. 1100-1160) and others warned their listeners that the Holy Spirit absented itself from the room of married folk performing the act even if for procreation alone. Celibacy thus soon became the badge of moral authority. However, this doctrine was not easy to implement. The problem was that a great many clerics entered the Church because it was their only way to pursue a professional career in law, administration, or scholarship. In 13th century England, one adult male in every 12 was a cleric. But that did not mean that one in every 12 had entered the Church to follow a religious vocation – or that this individual saw any need to suppress his sexual instincts. For most clerics, that is, the Church was simply a stepping stone to a professional career, imposing a "stained glass ceiling" upon themselves!

From the 7th to the 12th centuries, the Church continued to discuss what marriage actually was. Was it a moral contract? Did it have to be confirmed by sexual intercourse? The final judgment was that consent, not intercourse, makes marriage. The interesting phenomenon of syneisaktism, (spiritual marriage) whereby a married couple lived together but conducted themselves as brother and sister in the name of sexual abstinence proved an interesting development. Although it was a phenomenon of early Christianity, it is not unknown even today. This concept is, of course, unthinkable in Judaism.

Rigid theologians, however, tried to make life all the more difficult for married couples by recommending abstinence from sexual intercourse on Thursdays in memory of Christ's arrest, on Fridays in memory of his death, on Saturdays in honor of the Virgin Mary, on Sundays in honor of the resurrection, and on Mondays in commemoration of his death. In addition, there was also, of course, a ban on intercourse during holy days such as Easter, Pentecost, and Christmas! For good measure, abstinence was encouraged during the several days preceding communion!

Theologians recognized only one natural physical position for intercourse – the "missionary" position. All others positions were believed to be unnatural because they modeled man on the animals and so inverted the nature of male and female. Accordingly, competing positions were also suspected of preventing conception and thereby contrary to the very nature of marriage. However, the major sexual sin was contraception. Contraception, *coitus interruptus* along with both anal and oral intercourse created sins almost as heinous as homicide!

It was not until the 3$^{rd}$ century that the Church began to legislate against homosexuality. So much a part of the culture was pederasty that to legislate against homosexuality would be to alienate most of the clergy! In an environment in which one was not allowed to express his sexuality overtly without fear of condemnation, it was to be expected that clerics would express it covertly. Accordingly, in 567 the Second Council of Tours ruled that monks should never sleep two in a bed! Furthermore, to prevent the vile act, the Council decreed that dormitory lamps had to be kept burning all through the night.

Unfortunately, the rules of priestly celibacy did not achieve the desired results. Quite the opposite! Indeed, the sexual excesses of the priests of Rome were so bad that the Senate moved to expel them from the Roman Republic.

When Pope Paul V (ca 1550) sought suppression of licensed brothels in the Holy City, the Roman Senate petitioned against his carrying his concept into effect on the grounds that such brothels were the only means of hindering priests from violating their wives and daughters. In those days, it would seem, Rome was a *Holy City* in name only for there were 6,000 prostitutes in the *Holy City*, a city with a population of only 100,000.[10]

## BE CHASTE OR BE CAREFUL

The clergy commonly had mistresses, and convents were virtually houses of ill fame. A fish pond in Rome near a convent was drained by order of Pope Gregory. At the bottom were found 6,000 infant skulls, all victims of infanticide. Cardinal Peter d'Ailly (ca 1350-1420) confessed that he dared not describe the immorality of the nunneries. Albert the Magnificent, Archbishop of Hamburg, exhorted his priests: "*Si non caste, tamen caste*" (If you can't be chaste, at least be careful).

Another German bishop began to charge priests in his district a tax for each female they kept and for each child born. To his horror, he discovered that 11,000 women were kept by the priests of his diocese. Clearly, the problems arising from the rule of celibacy were too numerous to be ignored.

Although the major sexual sin was contraception, abortion within 40 days of conception – that is, before the fetus had acquired its human soul – was only fractionally less sinful.

St. Jerome proclaimed that a promiscuous woman who took potions to abort and then died went straight to Hell, branded as a three-fold murderess: as a suicide; as an adulteress to their heavenly bridegroom, Christ; and as a murderess of her still unborn child.

In the 13th century, Thomas Aquinas declared the following to be sexual sins in descending order of magnitude:

1. Bestiality
2. Homosexuality
3. Non-observance of the proper methods of coitus
4. Using artificial aids for stimulation
5. Anal or oral intercourse
6. Masturbation
7. Incest
8. Adultery
9. Seduction
10. Fornication

Thomas Aquinas argued in clerical hyperbole, that to empty the world of prostitutes would be to fill it with Sodomites. So the clergy took out shares in the houses of prostitution and gathered the girls tidily under their wings. Temple prostitutes flocked to Europe. And Avignon even offered a brothel in which girls spent part of their time serving God and the rest serving customers. But – Christians only! No Jews or heathens were permitted to cross the threshold. Pope Julius II was so impressed with the brothel at Avignon that in the early 15th century he founded one like it in the Holy City.

The 16th century, as we know it through Luther and others, was a time of Reformation. The reformers were intent upon clearing away the rubble and ruin of previous centuries and thus upon restoring a semblance of common sense and biblical truth. Arising as it did from the quagmire of ignorance and injustice, the Reformation could hardly move quickly. From the very beginning, it continued to focus on celibacy, marriage, and sexual sins. The reforming was made all the more difficult by the condom, which did not gain public acceptance until the 18th century.

The late 17th century and the 18th century was a period of fervent intellectual activity and often called the Enlightenment. It came to us through men such as Descartes and Voltaire. In its way, the Enlightenment was as iconoclastic as the Reformation. Curiosity, and therefore discovery, was unrestricted, even in the religious arena. One example relevant here, a definitive answer to a question unanswered for over 10,000 years: how does sexual intercourse produce children?

The 18th c and forward into the 19th c was, in general, a time for all sorts of absurd and inane claims. For example, Ellen White, (1827-1915) founder of the Seventh-Day Adventists, claimed that she had received a vision warning that masturbation would turn a man into a cripple and an imbecile. For some 50 years following, absurdly, the medical profession consistently and absurdly promised active masturbators the reward of blindness and epilepsy.

Unfortunately, I am sorry to report, almost everything taught in Christianity today and through the ages regarding sex, human sexuality has been and still is wrong, leading to mass sexual frustration and deeply rooted psychological bondage!

# CHAPTER 2
# MODERN THOUGHT

Have you ever wondered why some people think about sexuality as they do? All of us are sexual beings, with varying ways of expressing our sexuality. Why do we, individually and collectively, think of our sexuality as we do?

As a child growing up, I came from a large family. At one time there were five generations of us on both sides of my family living in one small area of Joplin, Missouri. My grandmother, my dad's mother, lived only two houses away. And her mother, my great grandmother, lived right across the street. Both of them had been widowed quite young. My grandfather passed away when he was only 40, leaving my grandmother widowed with three children. I often wondered why she never remarried.

I grew up as an only child until I was 17 when, at 42, my mother gave birth to my brother. When I found out she was pregnant, I was shocked – not that she was going to have a child; I just had no idea that my parents did...well, you know!

I slept in the same bed with them until I started grammar school at the age of 5. And I never heard them or anyone else in my extended family say anything about sex. Everything I had ever heard about sex came from someone at school. Only much later did I begin to wonder: why did my grandparents never remarry? I wondered why none of my other relatives ever mentioned the subject. Then, while studying the subject of sex education and therapy, I had a colleague give me an old book he had found in a used book store. This book answered some of my questions. The title: *Creative and Sexual Science: Manhood, Womanhood and their Mutual Interrelations. Love, Its Laws, Powers, etc., Selection or Mutual Adaptation, Courtship, Married life and Perfect Children* (1873) by Professor O.S. Fowler, Phrenology and Physiology. An inscription inside the book read, "To Sylvia and Edess – from Old Grandma Smith, Dr. Smith's Dr. Book."

Having been published after the Civil War and about 10 years before my grandmother was born, it exemplifies the state of sexual knowledge at that time in America. It is a hymn to utter ignorance. You can hardly believe what it proclaims. Not one thing in it is true:

> *Excerpts from Section II*
> *Secret Sins: Or Warning and Advice to Youth*
>
> *914. – Personal Fornication the worth of Sexual Vices*
>
> *Masturbation outrages nature's sexual ordinances more than any or all the other forms of sexual sin man can perpetuate, and inflicts consequences the most terrible. Would that its presentation 'might pass,' but 'sexual science' and the best good of man demand its fearless exposition.*

*It is man's sin of sins, and vice of vices; and has caused incomparably more sexual dilapidation, paralysis, and disease, as well as demoralization, than all the other sexual depravities combined. Neither Christendom nor heathendom suffers any evil at all to compare with this; because of its universality, and its terribly fatal ravages on body and mind; and because it attacks the young idols of our hearts, and hopes of our future years. Pile all other evils together – drunkenness upon all cheateries, swindling, robberies, and murders; and tobacco upon both, for it is the greater scourge; and all sickness, diseases and pestilences upon all; and war as the cap sheaf of them all – and all combined cause not a tithe as much human deterioration and misery as does this secret sin. Demand you a scientific warrant for an assertion thus sweeping and appalling? Find it in...Ho! Darling Youth! Please listen to a little plain talk from one who loves you with a father's affection.*

*If you were walking thoughtlessly along a pathway, across which was a deep, miry, miasmatic slough, so covered that you would not notice it till you had fallen in and defiled yourself all over with the filthiest, most nauseating slime possible, so that you could never cleanse yourself from this stench, and so that all who ever saw you would know what you had done; besides its being so poisonous as to destroy forever a large part of all your future life-enjoyment and capacities, and far more corrupting to your morals than blighting to health and happiness; would you not heartily thank any friend to kindly tell you plainly of your danger?*

*Such a danger, O splendid boy, O charming girl, awaits you: only that it is a thousand-fold worse than any description. It not only poisons your body, destroys your rosy cheeks, breaks down your nerves, impairs your digestion, and paralyzes your whole system; but it also corrupts your morals, creates thoughts and feelings the vilest and the worst possible, and endangers your very soul's salvation! No words can describe the miseries it inflicts throughout your whole life, down to death. But its ravages do not stop there. They follow and prey on you forever! You can never fully rid yourself of the terrible evils it inflicts. You may almost as well die outright as thus pollute yourselves.*

*The pathway of life you are now traveling is thus beset. This danger is the secret sin of self-pollution. It is by far the worst of all the sins and vices to which you are exposed. It blights nearly all. If it does not spoil you also, it will be because you heed this warning, and abstain wholly from it. Children, I pity you from the lowest depths of my soul, in view of the terrible ordeal before you; and rendered the more appalling by your ignorance of its evils.*

*It is called masturbation, and consists in indulging immodest feelings and actions, and imagining sexual pleasures with one of the opposite sex, whilst handling your own private parts.*[11]

## DR KELLOGG DEEMED SEX AS THE ULTIMATE ABOMINATION (CONTRIBUTED BY DR. RON MOSELEY)

Few activities are more entertaining than to investigate the health theories of Dr. John Harvey Kellogg, who gained a reputation as a nutritionist and sexual advisor at the Battle Creek Sanitarium in 1866.

The institution was originally the Western Health Reform Institute founded by Seventh Day Adventist leader Ellen G. White. As a doctor, Kellogg was noted for his eccentric ideas and methodologies, which he predicted would produce nothing short of a medical revolution.

By pumping yogurt cultures into the rectums of America's most wealthy, Kellogg claimed to cure cancer of the stomach, ulcers, diabetes, schizophrenia, manic depressives, acne, anemia, migraines and premature old age. Although the Battle Creek Vibratory Chair shook so violently that the pain it created originally appeared worse than the ailment, it stimulated the intestinal peristalsis and cured a variety of ills including headaches and back pain by supplying healthy oxygen to the body.

## SEX AND CORN FLAKES

Dr. Kellogg taught that almost all illness originated in the stomach and bowels, which he treated with repeated enemas in order to produce sparkling clean intestines. Kellogg held that virtually all other disease was a result of sexual intercourse. The eccentric therapies of the sanitarium included applying carbolic acid to the clitoris to prevent female masturbation, immersion in freezing radium-laced water, and electrical shock to some of the most sensitive parts of the body.

Among his drastic measures to rehabilitate masturbators, Dr. Kellogg regularly circumcised young boys without anesthetic noting that the brief pain would have a salutary effect upon the mind, especially if it was connected with the idea of punishment. Kellogg also assured that the soreness, which continued for weeks, would interrupt the practice leaving a memory firmly fixed and not soon forgotten.

The second treatment used by Kellogg to prevent masturbation included one or more silver sutures placed in such a manner as to prevent erection by drawing the foreskin over the glands and with a needle attaching a wire twisted together, which made it impossible for an erection to occur.

In female prevention of the solitary vice, Dr. Kellogg found that the application of pure carbolic acid (phenol) to the clitoris was an excellent means of allaying abnormal excitement. He also recommended bandaging or tying their hands, covering their genitals with patented cages, electrical shock, cool enemas, and the application of blisters and other irritants to the sensitive parts of the sexual organs in an effort to prevent children from the solitary vice (*Kellogg, Ladies Guide in Health and Disease*).

We laugh at such drivel today. But cry to think of the harm it wreaked upon anyone of my grandmother's generation who suffered the misfortune of reading and believing it.

In 1899, the popular temperance leader, Carrie A. Nation, displayed her disdain for the uses of alcohol and tobacco due to her first husband, which fueled a life of war against anything she considered evil. According to Nation, the six predominant evils included demon rum, corsets, tobacco, short skirts, Teddy Roosevelt and masturbation (*The Original Bar Room Smasher*, – reprint of Nation's book by the Kansas Museum of History, 2002.) Carrie Nation once wrote an article entitled *Mother Nation's Talk to Little Boys*, which suggested that masturbation was the cause for nearly everything from going blind to getting a first-class ticket to hell itself. Because of her preaching on the subject, Nation was arrested for violating the 1873 obscenity laws.

Samuel Langhorne Clemens (Mark Twain 1835-1910) gave a humorous speech to an all-male audience at the Stomach Club in Paris (1879) on the subject of *The Science of Onanism*, in which he quoted several authorities on the subject. Clemens quoted Benjamin Franklin as noting, "Masturbation is the best policy," and that the incontestable authority Brigham Young concluded, "As compared to the other thing, it is the difference between the lightning bug and lightning" (Clements, *Some Thoughts on the Science of Onanism*).

It is through the Christian theology of the first 1400-1500 years of Christianity and from books written by pseudo-scientists that people not only had some of the distorted and dangerous views about sex that they did but, as a result, continue to remain in ignorance and bondage until this very day.

It seems as though history may be repeating itself as a result of many of the things being written and said today by (let me remind you) people who are uncredentialed and/or have no training in the field. Be discerning as to what you read and to whom you listen. Make very sure that they are a recognized authority in the field. Remember, truth has a way of setting you free. Error has a way of bringing you into bondage.

# CHAPTER 3
# MARRIAGE

### THE BIBLE WAS A HEBREW DOCUMENT

Most people wouldn't think about going to Jewish material to study the subject of human sexuality. And yet the *Bible* in its entirety is a Hebrew document. In order to learn what the biblical position is on the subject, one has to examine it from a Hebrew perspective. But to do that, we have to look at it over a period of 3000 years!

To answer many of the questions one needs to understand that the *Bible* – in its entirety – is a Hebrew book. Jesus was not only was a Jew, he was a rabbi. He taught using well-known Jewish methods of instruction in the Hebrew language. Even those passages in the *New Testament* originally written in Greek have a Hebrew background as they are addressing Hebrew matters.

The late professor David Flusser wrote in *Jewish Sources in Early Christianity*:

This question of the spoken languages is especially important for understanding the doctrines of Jesus.

There are sayings of Jesus which can be rendered both into Hebrew and Aramaic; but there are some which can only be rendered into Hebrew, and none of them can be rendered only into Aramaic. One can thus demonstrate the Hebrew origins of the Gospels by retranslating them into Hebrew.

It appears that the earliest documents concerning Jesus were written works, taken down by his disciples after his death. Their language was early Rabbinic Hebrew with strong undercurrents of biblical Hebrew. Even in books of the *New Testament*, which were originally composed in Greek, such as the *Pauline Epistles*, there are clear traces of the Hebrew language; and the terminology in those books of the *New Testament*, which were composed in Greek, is often intelligible only when we know the original Hebrew terms. In these books, we can trace the influence of the Greek translation of the *Bible* side by side with the influence of the Hebrew original.[12]

Now, here is the point. If one is looking for a biblical or theological answer to a certain question, he or she must know the biblical position on this subject. One might well ask: "What was the position of Jesus or the other rabbis of his day on a given subject?" or "What does Judaism have to say about this subject or this issue?" The emphasis must be upon the Hebrew context.

## CREDIBILITY OF THE SOURCES
However, it was one thing to for me know Jewish history, culture, and law – and quite another talent to be proficient

in counseling, especially in sex education and therapy. Although my education in counseling and therapy was important, it was all the various fields of Hebrew studies that provided the best foundation for discussing what the Bible really teaches about sex, birth control, abortion, marriage, divorce, homosexuality, lesbianism, questionable gender, adultery, fornication, and masturbation – all important issues confronting our society today to the extent that some, such as abortion, have become hot potato political issues.

One might reasonably ask, "Why is knowledge of the biblical text or knowledge of Hebrew studies so important in dealing with these issues?" To answer that question, I want to quote from the Anglican author, Dr. D.S. Bailey:

> The Christian attitude to sexuality and/or its aspects was profoundly affected by the ascendancy of Hellenistic dualism over Hebraic naturalism during the first great age of the Church. The Jewish concepts of coitus, marriage and children, positive and affirmative within their inevitable limits were almost entirely over-laid by the Greco-Oriental tendencies to regard the good life as one essentially of ataraxia or impassive detachment from all that might impede the rational exercise of contemplation, and to look upon sexuality as something not only emotionally disturbing, but also in some sense defiling and tainted with evil. It is futile to speculate how Christian thought might have developed, in this and other realms of theology had the early Church clung more closely to its Hebraic roots.[13]

These Hebraic roots teach no antipathy to sex. Whatever the sin of Adam and Eve might have been, it was in no way connected with sexual activity. I shall address this point later – in more detail.

According to the biblical text and to Jewish Law, to marry and rear a family is a religious commandment. Indeed, it is at one with the commandment of *Genesis* 1:28, to be fruitful, to multiply and to fill the earth. Judaism declares that the unmarried person lives without joy, without blessing, and without good (*Yevamot* 62b). An unmarried man is not a man in the full sense. For it is said that "male and female created He them and blessed them and called their name man" (*Genesis* 5:2). Moreover, a wife meant a home, hence the saying a man's home is his wife (*Yoma* 1:1).

Rabbi Yossi said: "Never have I called my wife by that word, but always my home." (*Shab.* 118b)

The ideal of matrimony enjoined by the Talmud is of the highest. The ordinary term for marriage is *Kiddushin*, which means sanctification. It is so called because the husband prohibits his wife to the whole world like an object which is dedicated to the sanctuary. Other utterances advocating a lofty standard of domestic life are:

> He who loves his wife as himself honors her more than himself, leads his sons and daughters in the right path and arranges for their marriage soon after puberty. (*Yevamot* 62b)

> Honor your wife, thereby you enrich yourself. A man should be ever careful about the honor due his wife because no blessing is experienced in his house except on her account. (*B.M.* 59a)

> A man should spend less than his means on food and drink for himself, up to his means on his clothes, and above his means on honoring his wife and children, because they are dependent upon him, while he is dependent upon Him who spake and the Universe came into being. (*Chul.* 84b)

Husband and wife are exhorted to look upon each other as partners in life. Therefore, the proverb urged if your wife is short, bend down and whisper to her (*B.M.* 59a). In other words, the man should not think himself too superior to consult his wife on his affairs.

Once married, the woman is due certain rights. Once married, the Mitzvah of *Onah*, or conjugal dues, rests upon the man. In *Exodus* 21:10, the husband's obligations are specified as *sh-er, k-sut*, and *onah* (her food, clothing, and sexual rights). The equation here of the woman's sexual rights with food and clothing as basic necessities of life has led a modern writer to say that no more eloquent testimony to the importance of legitimate sex among the ancient Hebrews could be imagined.[14]

Actually, the law goes further in that a prenuptial agreement by the woman to forgo her claims to sexual rights is not to be recognized while such an agreement against food and clothing may be. According to Jewish Law (*Keth* 5:6), a man is required to have sexual relations with his wife so many times per week based upon his profession: for men of leisure or independent means, every day; for ordinary workmen, twice a week; for ass drivers, once a week; for camel drivers, once every 30 days; for sailors, once every six months.

If a man refuses or refrains from his conjugal dues, the woman can add to her marriage settlement three dinars per week. Conversely, if the woman refuses in her conjugal responsibilities, the man may reduce her marriage settlement by seven dinars each week until it reaches the full amount of her marriage settlement, at which time he could send her away with nothing. Today, if the husband is negligent in his conjugal responsibilities, the wife can take him to Rabbinic Court and be granted a divorce plus alimony.

One important note is that the *Mitzvah of Onah* involves the how as well as the when. The purpose of the sexual relation is that one body may take and find pleasure in the other (*shaguf neheneh min haguf*). A man is required to give joy (*Lesammeah*) to his wife in the manner of the *Mitzvah*. The quality of the *Onah* is as important as the act itself. Nothing demonstrates this point better than this excerpt from a document of marriage entitled *Iggeret Hakodesh* or the *Epistle of Holiness*. It is a letter written by Rabbi Moses ben Nahman, also called Nachmanides (d. 1270). In the sixth chapter entitled "On the Quality of the Act" the author has this to say:

> Engage her first in conversation that puts her heart and mind at ease and gladdens her. Thus your mind and your intent will be in harmony with hers. Speak words which arouse her to passion, oneness, love, desire and eros, and words which elicit attitudes of reverence for God, piety, and modesty. Tell her of pious and good women who gave birth to fine and pure children. Speak with her words – some of love, some of erotic passion, some of piety and reverence.
>
> Never may you force her, for in such union the divine presence cannot abide. Your intent is then different from hers and her mood is not in accord with yours. Quarrel not with her nor strike her in connection with this act, as our sages taught just as a lion tramples and devours and has no shame, so a boorish man strikes and copulates and has no shame. Rather, win her over with words of graciousness and seductiveness.
>
> Hurry not to arouse passion until her mood is ready. Begin in love. Let her semination take place first.[15]

The word semination refers to female orgasm. Orgasm first appeared in medical literature in the late 19th century.

The point here is that the husband's obligation to *Onah* is not as great as his assuring the woman's sexual satisfaction, and this point surely applies to technique in the modern sense. When asked by prospective bridegroom whether the Mitzvah of *Onah* implies that he should study books on how intercourse should properly be performed in a matter pleasing to his wife and conducive to domestic peace, the Rabbi answered in the affirmative.

May I remind you and emphasize that the husband has a responsibility to his wife in the matter of sexual relations. He needs to go to whatever lengths necessary to ensure her sexual satisfaction. One of the first and most important steps is communication. Converse with her about her likes and dislikes, study something about the female body. An excellent resource book probably easily available from either Amazon or AbeBooks.com is entitled simply, *ABC's of the Human Body*, by Reader's Digest. It discusses not only understanding the female body but many other important subjects. Many other related subjects relating to the human body and one's overall health and wellbeing are addressed as well.

Discuss openly and honestly about her likes and dislikes. Communicate. Remember there is absolutely nothing wrong with fantasies and/or fetishes or experimentation; all is legitimate and acceptable as long as both parties are agreeable, it is safe, pleasurable, no one is being hurt, and both parties are finding pleasure and fulfillment in one another. If it should happen – after open and honest discussion with your partner – that you might seem to have irreconcilable differences, it may be time for you to seek out a legitimate, certified sex therapist who can offer assistance and wise counsel.

Before concluding, I believe that it is appropriate to say a word or two on the subject of abstinence only programs.

Recently, in certain southern states they are now discussing the subject of Abstinence-Plus programs, meaning teaching abstinence plus sexual education. Until recent times such was not needed for a number of reasons – different mores, a different outlook on both sex and marriage. Early marriage was encouraged: just 12 or 13 for the girls and 18 for the boys. By the time their hormones were raging, there was a normal and acceptable outlet available for them.

Times have changed, and early marriage is no longer practiced nor condoned – at least in the United States. It is certainly no solution at all to assume that our youth today are going to follow any kind of abstinence only program when their sexuality is raging like a fire down inside. Why do we allow ourselves to be blinded by hyper religious naiveté when what is needed is realistic and age-appropriate program of sex education, starting about the $5^{th}$ or $6^{th}$ grade and taught by certified and/or credentialed instructors in the field.

Young people need at an early age to be educated as to the consequences of their actions – not only for themselves but for others as well. They need instructions not about sin but on ethics and morals and that their actions will have everlasting consequences. Yet who is ultimately responsible for it? Parents need to step up to the plate and be responsible for the care and education of their children.

I know that it is difficult to get through to young people when their sexual hormones are raging inside of them. Sometimes visual evidence may make more of an impression than just mere words so that it may be prudent and possible to discuss the general subject of sexually transmitted diseases and illustrate with visual materials. There are many different sexually transmitted diseases, but several need to be especially stressed because of the insidious nature of the disease itself; such as, Chlamydia, which in many instances has no immediate symptoms, HPV or the human papilloma virus which causes genital warts.

Unfortunately, there are dozens of strains of HPV and some of the more malignant strains can lead to cervical cancer. Herpes is another, plus there is now an antibiotic-resistant strain of gonorrhea. Ideally, sex education would begin in the home and information children receive at school would be an affirmation and extension of the education they receive in their home. I want to emphasize one point however – before parents can educate their children and set the proper example, they must educate themselves.

If the parents and the educational system do not provide them with the information they need, not only will the children suffer, but society, as a whole, will have to suffer as well.

## CHAPTER 4
## ORGASM

Because such an emphasis has been placed upon orgasm in the *Epistle of Holiness*, I think it appropriate for me to offer a few words on the subject. Recent statistics suggest fewer than 50 percent of women achieve orgasm through vaginal intercourse. In most instances, it is not a problem with the woman but, unfortunately, a problem with the man. In many, if not most instances, men simply do not know what to do. (For purposes of visual reference in this chapter, we have inserted illustrations of both the female and male reproductive systems as Appendix I and Appendix II.)

It has been said that the object of lust is orgasm. In recent times, sex therapists have demystified orgasm. We know there are four phases in intercourse: excitement, plateau, orgasm, and resolution. In men at orgasm, there is a contraction of the rectal sphincter at .8-second intervals along with a reduction of voluntary muscle control, resulting in involuntary muscle spasms throughout the body and ending in ejaculation followed by a series of swift involuntary rhythmic muscular contractions in the penis, testes, and nearby areas. This forces semen from the penis and the first three or four contractions occur at .8-second intervals.

In women, the signs are similar. At orgasm, there are contractions of the uterus, vagina, and rectal sphincter again at .8-second intervals during which the woman may or may not experience ejaculation. The principal difference being that, in males, sperm are emitted upon ejaculation. Orgasm will usually last three to ten seconds. But it can last one minute or longer in females, especially if they lose consciousness.

The real question, however, is not how but why. Why orgasm?

Evolutionary theorists suggest that female orgasm was adaptive. It served an important role in assuring the survival of the offspring for it helped solidify the pair-bond between the parents. Females who wanted their offspring to survive benefitted greatly from promiscuity. Males can choose to protect and care for their offspring or they can kill them – depending upon whether or not they think they are the father. The female who can persuade the community of males to protect her offspring stands a better chance of passing on her genes. The more males with whom she can mate, the more the chances the offspring will survive. Therefore, the female establishes a network of males to ensure the survival of her offspring. If the male thinks he is the father, he will go to great lengths to protect his offspring. But how to draw multiple partners into this net of possible paternity?

The female needs a motivation to solicit and mate with the maximum number of male partners. That motivation is orgasm. Each partner with whom she mates increases the possibility for the survival of her offspring. This theory jibes well with the findings of Masters & Johnson. Women remain sexually excitable after orgasm and maintain a more prolonged arousal than men.

Of course, it is all theory and the beauty of the theory is that we can make up one of our own. But most of us don't really care about the why. We want to know about the how. And to know about the how, we must first know about the different kinds of female orgasm. Recently it has been suggested that there are as many as 25 different kinds of orgasm possible. We are going to look briefly at only five of these. The five are vaginal, clitoral, anal, tactile (skin or touch) and suggestive.

Many women fail to realize that orgasm in women is essentially a learned response. This means that the center of female orgasm is between her ears. The mind, that is, controls orgasm. Recent research has linked the ability to have orgasm with the brain. Some interesting research on the subject has taken place and continues to be ongoing. You can find additional information on the ongoing research online: Just simply type into your search engine, *orgasm and the brain*.

In vaginal orgasm, five muscle groups link together to elicit orgasm: the adductor, the sphincter, the pelvic, the pubic, and the pubbococcogeal. To achieve vaginal orgasm, all of these muscles must be working together. In vaginal orgasm, the penis thrusts the muscles and hits the cervix, the womb rotates, the muscles tighten, the clitoris is stimulated, and orgasm results. If the pubbococcogeus is weak, vaginal orgasm will be difficult. The pubbococcogeus may be weakened by childbirth or by an episiotomy. Today's sex therapists routinely recommend against a woman having an episiotomy. The husband, the nurse, or the health-care professional may use certain massage techniques to relax and stretch the pubbococcogeus. Exercises, such as the Kegel exercise, may assist in strengthening the pubbococcogeus.

Don't be afraid to position yourself for the deepest penetration, or to try different positions. If one has a small clitoris, one may need to position oneself on top – don't be afraid to take charge. Don't be afraid to experiment. Don't be afraid to say "harder" or "faster." It is vital that you study your own body and share your findings with your partner. Don't be afraid to share with your partner what you want, what feels good, and what you like.

## FIRST THINGS FIRST

Remember, men, what Nachmanidies had to say in the *Epistle of Holiness.* Do not hurry. Let her semination, i.e., orgasm, take place first. In other words, be considerate!

By now, surely everyone has heard of the "G-spot," named after the German scholar Ernst Grafenberg who first called attention to it. It is seemingly a vestige of the male prostate gland. It is embedded in the upper vaginal wall about even with the pubic hairline. A woman can definitely tell when it has been located and stimulated, for it feels quite different from any other spot in the vagina. Often, when stimulated, it elicits orgasm and even ejaculation.

All this becomes especially relevant when we discuss the center of orgasmic response. Most women are capable of having an orgasm when the clitoris is stimulated either manually or orally. If the woman is orgasmic both vaginally and clitorally, she will usually declare that the clitoral orgasm is the more powerful because of its extreme sensitivity, as it corresponds to the male glans penis. However, many women claim that the clitoral climax is less satisfying or fulfilling. Not all clitorises are the same. Some are small, some are large and some embedded. The man may not know precisely where it is and even the woman may not know. In that case, the Web site, en.wikipedia.org/wiki/Clitoris may prove helpful.

## A HIDDEN WEAPON BETWEEN YOUR EARS

The clitoris is not the center of orgasmic response. We know this because many transsexuals who have undergone surgical realignment have no clitoris and yet most are quite orgasmic. We know, too, because the center for our orgasmic response is actually between the ears!

Some women, because of childbirth, or perhaps because of an episiotomy, have such a weak pubbococcogeus that they attempt orgasm through anal intercourse. There shouldn't be any mystery about this, for the nerves eliciting orgasm are the same. They are the same nerves that elicit the orgasm vaginally.

However, I want to urge caution because the tissue in the anus and rectum is not designed for penal thrusting as was the vagina. Moreover, the anus and the rectum are hardly sterile environments! You must, then, practice sound hygiene. Never switch from the anus to the vagina without washing thoroughly. Always use a water-based lubricant with a condom preferably water-based and not baby oil or mineral oil, as dangerous diseases can pass through even latex condoms when the wrong lubricant is used. For maximum safety, always use a latex condom.

Skin or touch – Remember, the center of orgasmic response is between the ears. The mind controls orgasm.

As mentioned previously, the G-spot is a mass of tissue located on the anterior vaginal wall at the pubic hair line. When directly stimulated, it elicits a sensation that may lead to orgasm and even ejaculation. Seemingly, this mass of tissue is a vestige of the male prostate gland. It may simply lie over a deep part of the clitoris. The "legs" of the *crura* come together in the deep anterior wall of the vagina. The Internet can become your best source of information on the subject of the G-spot. The point here is that the female body is marvelously designed, like a magnificent, finely tuned instrument. The artist who knows how to play that instrument can make beautiful music. When any part of the body is stimulated through light touch in the right places, a woman will usually feel sensations in the area of the "G-spot."

The woman who is in touch with her sexuality and willing to spend the time and effort to experiment will find that she is capable of orgasm through almost any part of her body because the center of the orgasmic response lies between her ears.

Not all orgasms are the same. On a scale of 1 to 10, some may be a 3 or 4; some, an 8-10. Then some may even be wall-bangers. The key is learning to relax – sharing feelings in general and fears in particular.

Today, dozens of sex manuals and books are available. In this connection, I have two suggestions: I recommend that you consult more than one text. I further think that you should buy secular-oriented guides, meaning texts written by certified sex educators and/or therapists and directed toward the general reader rather than texts written by religious authors and directed toward a given religious group. (Examples of such texts appear in the bibliography. I draw widely on many of them in this work.)

In his *Epistle of Holiness*, Nachmanides advises: "know that sexual intercourse is holy and pure when carried on properly in the proper time and with the proper intentions,"[16] contrary to certain Christian denominational admonition.

Nachmanides explains that the pious Jew prefers Friday night for marital love. "Understand, therefore," he adds, "that the pious have not selected the week days on which physical activity predominates for their marital relations. They prefer the Sabbath which is spiritual, holy unto the Lord. The holy person performs an act of holiness at a time of holiness." This statement again illustrates the contrast between Christian and Jewish thought on sex.[17]

## CHAPTER 5
# JUDAIC THOUGHT ON HUMAN SEXUALITY

Herman Wouk, in the book *This Is My God*, makes this observation concerning the Jewish sexual outlook:

> What in other cultures has been a deed of shame or of comedy or of orgy or of physical necessity or of high romance has been in Judaism one of the main things God wants men to do. If it also turns out to be the keenest pleasure in life, that is no surprise to a people eternally sure that God is good.[18]

This material speaks for itself. It should not be necessary to add a single expository word to demonstrate that a Judeo/Christian sexual ethic is, at the very least, a fallacy in concept. But all of this raises one basic question: *What is and what is not acceptable intercourse? What constitutes normal intercourse?*

The one imperative is that mutual pleasure is present in the sexual act. So, how do we know this? Simply because Jewish literature describes the sexual act as the heterosexual relationship in which *guf neheneh min haguf* applies. That is, each body derives pleasure from the other. In the 12th century book, *Sefer Hasidim (The Book of the Pious),* requires that, whatever the practice, the wife's comfort and approval must be consulted. The husband must consult the wife concerning her comfort and approval. What, then, would be legally banned or unnatural intercourse?

Regarding the matter of unnatural intercourse, three variations have been suggested:[19]

*Hi lemalah* – the dorsal position; woman on top.

*Panim Keneged oref or derekh mekom hatashmish meahorayim* – retro; the man entering from behind,

*Pi hatabaat* – literally, the mouth of the ring, referring to either oral or anal sex.

The general ruling is for a man to do with his wife what he will. And all so-called unnatural acts are permitted – if both parties agree to them. Note that procreation need not be the motive.

Rabbi Joseph asserts that clothing, one of the three provisions a husband owes to his wife, is sexually symbolic. It symbolizes the closeness of the flesh. So, the conjugal act must relate directly to the flesh. Rabbi Joseph adds that, even if couples – for religious modesty – wear clothes during the sex act as did the Pagan Persians, this is counter to love and could constitute cause for divorce.

The sexual aspect of marriage does not fall under the shadow of sin or shame. The wife is urged to use cosmetics, wear jewelry, and the like so that she will always continue to be attractive to her husband. Maharam Rotenberg threatens: "let a curse descend upon a woman who has a husband and does not strive to be attractive for him."

Judaism is not Puritanism. *Ecclesiastes* warns: "Do not be overly religious." (*Ecclesiastes* 7:16) In this connection, one's sexual life is his or her own. The bedroom door should, figuratively speaking, stay locked. Sex is intimate by its very nature and, so, necessarily private. There is a Hebrew word used for sexual intimacy, *yichud*, which means privacy.

## CHAPTER 6
# CONTRACEPTION OR BIRTH CONTROL

If the biblical view of marital sex affirms the legitimacy of pleasure as a function or as the objective, what does this say about the use of a contraceptive device? An answer appears, with minor variations, six times in Jewish literature. It is a homily of sorts, the *Baraita of the Three Women*. *Baraita* means *outside* and refers to the fact that the text lies outside the official *Mishnah*, or oral law, but derives from the time thereof. The passage reads:

> Rabbi Bebai recited before Rabbi Nahman – Three categories of women must use a *mokh* in marital intercourse – a minor, a pregnant woman, and a nursing mother. The minor because, otherwise, she might become pregnant and die. A pregnant woman because she might cause her fetus to become a *sandal*, which refers to the probability of a dual pregnancy. A nursing woman because she might have to wean her child prematurely and it would

die. And, what is a minor, from the age of 11 years and a day until the age of 12 years and a day. One who is under or over this age carries on her marital intercourse in the usual manner.[20]

The word *mokh* derives from the root meaning "to crush" or "to soften" and denotes a tuft of wool or cotton. As such, it was a medieval tampon. However, other absorbent devices could also serve, such as a sea sponge. In any event, birth control devices have never been a moral issue in Jewish life.

Seneca, (4 BCE-65 CE), once declared in a remark later incorporated into Christian doctrine: "Nothing is fouler than to love a wife like an adulteress. One ought to act with his wife as a husband, not a lover, and ought to imitate the beasts who do not mate when pregnant." Origen in the 2nd century as well as Jerome in the 4th, advanced Seneca's teaching on this point. Both considered coitus during pregnancy to be lechery and shame in large part because of supposed danger to the fetus.

In the Jewish tradition, for several reasons, sexual intercourse is recommended during pregnancy. This was to advance the psychological well-being of the mother, especially in the final trimester.

Today of course, various birth-control devices are available. Diaphragm, condom, spermicides, douching, the IUCD (intrauterine contraceptive device), and the pill are available. Today, the pill seems the least objectionable method of birth control.

Another point for consideration is that of sexual responsibility. The *Mitzvah* of *Onah* is incumbent upon the husband. The husband must be alert to the mood and gestures of his wife. He needs to learn how to *read* her. Marital relations are integral to the recreational side of marriage and to *shlom bayyit* (the peace of the home). If procreation or the conception of children would be detrimental to the wife's health, contraception would be mandated. Contrary to Catholic and other Christian denominational teaching, the use of birth control devices in Judaism, and the biblical position as well, would be not only permissible, but, in some instances, laudatory.

## CHAPTER 7
## ABORTION

Over the past 20 years or so, the subject of abortion has filtered over into the political arena. It is an emotional subject with pro-life advocates on one side and pro-choice on the other. Few have mentioned the third possibility. Both could be wrong!

The Christian doctrine on abortion is founded on neither Roman nor Hebrew law. Rather, on Greek law. That is, the doctrine of the Pythagorean Greeks says the soul enters the body at conception which prevailed in Christianity. Such was the doctrine of Tertullian (155-220) as well in the $3^{rd}$ century of the present era. And it was later confirmed by St. Gregory of Nyssa (335-394) in the $4^{th}$ century. But, in the $5^{th}$ century, Augustine declared that only a formed fetus, one of 40 days or more, has a soul.

Saint Fulgentius declared that all infants, whether they die in their mother's womb or after, must be baptized in the name of the Father, the Son, and the Holy Ghost or they will be punished in everlasting fire. For even though they have no sin of their own, they carry with them the condemnation of Original Sin from the moment of conception. Judaism espouses no such theology and, once again, Jewish and Catholic doctrines part company.

The subject is a very emotional one. Accordingly, most people think about it with their hearts rather than their heads. But we must think about it with our heads: rationally, conceptually and probingly. The basic difference between Jewish Law on the one hand, and ancient Greek and Roman law on the other regarding this subject, is vital.

Jewish law is ethical whereas Greek and Roman law is political. Politics subjugates the good of the individual to the good of the state. Ethics does the reverse. The political state knows military units and taxpayers. The ethical state knows persons.

Let's consider a few relevant points:

1. First of all, there is life in the sperm and in the egg. (Life is defined as the condition that distinguishes organisms from inorganic objects and dead organisms, being manifested by growth through metabolism, reproduction, and the power of adaptation to environment through changes originating internally.[21]) There is life even before the moment of conception!
2. After conception, the union of the sperm with the egg is, for the first 40 days, an embryo. It is a mass or growth within the woman that is either potentially benign or potentially malignant.
3. After 40 days, it becomes more: a fetus. But it does not become a human being until it draws its first breath outside the womb.[22]

If, at any time during the pregnancy, the fetus poses a threat to the well-being of the mother, abortion is permissible according to the rabbinic authorities or, in some cases, even mandated.

For centuries, rabbinic authorities have equated mental health with physical health. A responsum dated 1913 applied specifically to the matter of abortion in which mental health risk was equated to physical health risk. A woman who is in danger of losing her mental health would qualify for a termination of the pregnancy.

Additionally, danger to the health of an existing child serves as justification for termination. For example, a woman who had an infant child but lacked sufficient milk to support an additional infant and could not substitute formula feeding, termination would be justified to protect the health of the existing child.

Of course, in cases of rape the assumption is that the pregnancy may certainly be terminated. Although the woman is considered the vehicle for reproduction, i.e., Mother Earth, she differs from Mother Earth in that she need not nurture seed implanted within her against her will. She may uproot seed illegally sown.

However, I hasten to add that blanket abortion or abortion on demand would be unacceptable by almost all rabbinic authorities.

Rabbi Uziel declares: "It is clear that abortion is not permitted without reason. That would be destructive and frustrative of the possibility of life. But, for reason, even if it is a slim reason, such as to prevent suffering, either physical or mental, then we have precedent and authority to permit it."[23] That principle was carried forward and remains the basic principle today.

But, that raises another question. What if the child is born with a severe disability and is doomed to a less-than-normal life? Since we really would not know how challenged that less-than-normal life would be and since no permission exists in Jewish law to kill children born with a disability, permission simply on these grounds would be denied. However, if an abortion for that same potentially deformed fetus were sought on the grounds of causing severe anguish to the mother, permission would be granted.

The potential of the fetus is unknown. By contrast, the present life of the mother is known and she is requesting consideration and compassion based upon her fear that continuing the pregnancy would have a debilitating effect, psychologically and/or otherwise. On this basis, termination would be justified.

An additional point for consideration relates to a woman who might seek to render herself sterile because childbearing has been unusually painful. The ruling is that such would be allowed because no woman is required to build up the world by destroying herself. As mentioned previously, blanket abortion would certainly not be allowed and in every instance the woman would be enjoined to discuss her situation and condition with medical and/or spiritual authorities. But the basic ruling is that the woman has the right over her own body. Accordingly, a humane compassion for the welfare of the woman would move the rabbinic authorities to be guided by the principle that her pain comes first.

Admittedly, the subject of abortion is an emotional one. Few realize that the Church and religious belief has largely perpetuated this subject. Recently, a Web site posted an opinion on the subject of abortion declaring that a child in the womb is a human person. They extrapolate that because the *Bible* says, "Thou shalt not kill," killing a human person is, therefore wrong, meaning that abortion is killing a human person, thus abortion is wrong! This is the typical religious perspective on this subject. Not only is it naïve and poor biblical exegesis, but it is just flat out wrong.

Notice item #3 above, that the fetus is not considered a human person until it draws its first breath outside of the womb. Until that time, it is considered only as potential life.

Secondly, the *Bible* does not say, "*Thou shalt not kill*" as in this circumstance. The term in Hebrew means you shall not commit premeditated murder. All Halachic (Jewish Law) scholars agree that abortions performed in order to preserve the life of the mother are not only permissible but mandatory. The stage of the pregnancy does not matter. If there is a question as to the life of the mother or that of the unborn child, the Law always rules in favor of the mother.

It is time for us to take a step backward and look at the subject from a reasonable and rational perspective rather than an emotional one or religious one. Since each case is different, each case should be looked at on its own merits rather than lumping every case and/or condition together. The physical and/or mental condition of the mother deserves our first consideration. This is not an issue for political debate or political platform. It is an issue for education, for understanding and for common sense.

The subject of abortion should certainly not be a political or religious one. Our government, both at the State and Federal level as well as all religious institutions should be just as concerned, if not more so, about the vast numbers of children who are being born today who are orphaned or abandoned, uncared for and with little or no hope for the future. Over one million children died of hunger in Africa alone last year. That total could be added to the millions of additional children in other third-world countries around the world.

Governments and religious institutions around the world should be concerned about these vast numbers of children who are orphaned or abandoned and ignored and pose tremendous potential problems for their community or state or government where they live and are trying to grow up on the streets, ignored and alone.

Our government should be equally concerned about the number of women who continue to get pregnant, time after time, simply to add to their welfare check. It might be a financial benefit for the mother, but the children certainly pose additional problems for society as well as increasing the financial burden upon taxpayers. Although these children will continue to pose potential problems, the government programs that incentivize this pattern of behavior must change or we are going to continue to bear the financial, societal and economic burden. An intelligent solution must be found. If governments and religious institutions are going to focus their attention some place, then let it be focused where it will do the maximum good for the maximum number of people.

## CHAPTER 8
# MARRIAGE LAWS AND CUSTOMS

### AGE, PURPOSE, IDEALS

To marry and to rear a family was a positive religious commandment. *Proo urvoo oomilu et haaretz* (*Genesis* 1:28) translated as "Be fruitful, multiply and fill the earth." A wife meant a home; hence the saying, *a man's home is his wife*. Rabbi Yossi said, "Never have I called my wife by that word but always my home." Early marriage was advocated for males at age 18. (*Avot* 5:21) It was the father's duty to secure a husband for his daughter at an early age – roughly, at age 13 or 14. According to Talmudic law, it was forbidden to give one's daughter in marriage while she was still a minor. If one should do so, when she reached the age of 12 the marriage could be annulled without a divorce. The *Talmud* encouraged: "go marry one who is about your own age and do not introduce strife into your house."

Rabbinic law declared: "a man is forbidden to take a woman to wife without having first seen her, lest he afterwards perceive in her something objectionable and she becomes repulsive to him."

The principal purpose of marriage was the rearing of a family. It was enjoined that a man should sell all he possesses in order to marry the daughter of a learned man. The ideal was for the father to train his sons to be learned scholars and to give his daughter in marriage to a scholar. The father was advised "not to allow his son to marry the daughter of an ignoramus." The ideal of marriage is of the highest, and the common term is *kiddushin* – denoting sanctification.

Here are a few kindred comments:

Husbands and wives must look upon each other as partners as well as lovers.

The man should not hold himself so far above his wife as not to consult her on matters affecting both.

Both the *Bible* and the *Talmud* sanctioned polygamy. A man could have as many wives as he wanted as long as he could adequately support and care for them. However, one authority declared he may not exceed four. In addition, he was allowed any number of concubines. One order (or chapter) in the *Mishnah*, *Order Nashim* (women), contains various laws relating to the fellow wife – or, as she was known, the co-wife.

Additionally, there was no injunction against a man going to a prostitute as long as that prostitute was not a cult prostitute associated with some pagan deity.

By the 10th century, the practice of polygamy had begun to unravel as the result of a ban put on polygamy by Rabbi Gershom Ben Judah. This ban was to last only until 1240 CE although because no mention can be found of this in existing sources the ban is still in force mainly in the Ashkenazi communities although it was not accepted among the Sephardic and/or the Oriental communities. This was apparently because in those countries where Ashkenazi Jewry formed the main part of the community as it did in Europe and America, polygamy was forbidden by the dominant religion, Christianity, and, therefore, by the secular law. This was not the case in the oriental countries and, thus, Maimonides, who was a Sephardic Jew, makes no reference at all to the ban.

It is interesting when people move from a country where the ban was in place to a country where it was not, the ban adhered to the individual and accompanied him from place to place so that he always remained subject to it. And too, local custom is followed so that if the ban applies to a particular country, it is binding on everyone irrespective of their country of origin. If, on the other hand, a man legally married two wives in a country where it was permitted, he was not obliged to divorce either of them after arriving in another country where the ban was in force. This same custom applies in the land of Israel until today.

## THE SIGNIFICANCE OF THE TALMUD

Originally, Jewish scholarship was oral and the interpretations were meticulously passed down to future generations. When the Jews were driven from Jerusalem, during the Babylonian Exile, the non-Jewish kings permitted the rabbis to maintain their interpretations by incorporating Jewish academies, while absent from Jerusalem. The situation dramatically changed following the destruction of Jerusalem in 70 CE, when the Temple was destroyed and the Jews were scattered and by 135 CE, driven from Jerusalem. By 200 CE, the original Jewish interpretations were in danger of being lost or changed by Jews living outside the land and culture of Israel. It is during the Rabbinic Period that ancient interpretations began to be recorded in writing. Although the Talmudic and Mishnaic literature was not perfect, it has remained the earliest and most reliable view into what ancient Jewish believers understood to be truth concerning biblical interpretation.

## DISSOLUTION OR DIVORCE

Despite precautions, couples often found themselves ill-mated. Thus it was a common saying: "among those who will never behold the face of Gehinnom is he who has a bad wife." Among those whose "life is not life" is the man who is ruled by his wife. Under the law of the *Talmud*, if husband and wife wish to separate there was no difficulty in dissolving the marriage: a bad wife is like leprosy to her husband. What is the remedy? Let him divorce her and be cured of his leprosy. It was even asserted that, if one has a bad wife, it was a religious duty to divorce her.

Something now of the utmost importance – in the 1$^{st}$ century various rabbinical schools or academies arose. One was the School of Shammai. Another was the School of Hillel and, of course, the School of Jesus (See Glossary for the School of Hillel, School of Shammai). Hillel and Shammai took opposite views of *Deuteronomy* 24:1, which allows a man to send away his wife if she *finds no favor in his eyes* because he has found some *unseeming thing* in her. The phrase *unseeming thing* denotes literally in Hebrew, the nakedness of a thing. The School of Shammai explained this to mean that a man may not divorce his wife unless he has discovered her to be unfaithful. The School of Hillel, on the other hand, understood this phrase to mean that he may divorce her even if she spoiled his food by poor cooking. From the words *if she finds no favor in his eyes*, Rabbi Akiva argued that he may divorce her even if he has found another woman more beautiful than she.

## ADULTERY AND FORNICATION

To the School of Hillel and the School of Shammai can be

added a third school – the School of Jesus – as all three schools are contemporary. If one does not understand that these three schools are frequently at odds with one another, he/she will misunderstand much in the words of Jesus. For example, in the story in *John* 8:3-11 about the woman who had been taken in adultery.

> The Pharisees brought the woman to Him and set her in His midst. (*John* 8:3)

> They said, "Moses commanded us that she should be stoned. What do you say?" (*John* 8:5)

> They said this tempting Him in order that they might accuse him. But Jesus stooped down and wrote something with his finger on the ground. (*John* 8:6)

It is impossible to know what he wrote. But since they invoke Moses and the commandment in the Law, I would suggest that he wrote *Lo Tinaf*, which is translated "you shall not commit adultery." But adultery in both thought and meaning denotes something quite different than commonly assumed in English.

Ibn Ezra, a medieval Spanish commentator (1089-1164) asserts that the statement refers to all illicit relations as outlined in *Leviticus* 18:6-30. A man was forbidden to marry:

> Anyone not of the Jewish faith,

> The daughter of an adulterous or incestuous union,

> A married woman until all divorces have been completed,

His own divorced wife after her marriage to another man and the latter's death or divorce,

The widow of a childless husband who is survived by a brother until after the *chalitzah* ceremony has been performed,

A married woman with whom he has committed adultery,

A *Kohen* (priest) may not marry a divorced woman, a *chalitzah* widow, a convert, a *zonah* (prostitute), a *chalalah* (female offspring of a *Kohen* with a woman who is forbidden to him because he is a *Kohen*),

Relatives, such as mother, grandmother, step mother, daughter, granddaughter, daughter-in-law, sister, half-sister, brother's wife, aunt, uncle's wife, etc.

With this background at hand we can now understand a little more when Jesus stood up and said unto them,

"Now whichever one of you has not done this, you cast the first stone." And they all turned and left leaving Jesus and the woman alone.

And Jesus said unto her, "Woman, where are your accusers? Is there no one here to condemn you?"

And she said, "No, Lord."

And Jesus said, "Neither do I condemn you. Go and sin no more."

Her accusers had fled because all of them were perhaps guilty of violating one or more of the prohibitions listed in *Leviticus* 18:6-30.

It was the hallmark of the Jewish marriage to look for the ideal mate. Modesty was the foundation of Jewish values, which meant discrete habits, quiet speech, dignity, discretion, and avoidance of grossness and raucous behavior.

In *The Poisoning of Eros* (1989), Raymond J. Lawrence, Jr., an Episcopal clergyman, asserts:

> The biblical commandment against adultery has little to do with sex as such, has nothing to do with monogamy and certainly has nothing to do with sexual purity as an ideal. The invasion or intrusion into a private domain and contravention of an existing covenant is the concern that motivates the *Torah's* prohibition of adultery. As Paul Lehman points out, the commandment means *thou shalt not break in and break up a marriage.* The Jews were concerned that the community respect and protect marital covenants.[24]

Lawrence further urges:

> Following the spirit of the Talmudic tradition, we should attend to the political dimension of any sexual liaison. A particular act of adultery, therefore, stands under moral judgment only to the extent of its political malfeasance.[25]

Another puzzling passage in this regard appears in *Matthew* 19:9 where Jesus declares:

> Whosoever shall put away his wife except it be for fornication and shall marry another, commits

adultery. And whosoever marries her which is put away, commits adultery.

What does that passage mean? If you are not acquainted with Jewish law, you have no idea.

In biblical days, and even today in certain cultures, the virginity of the bride is a prized commodity. As previously mentioned, in many Eastern countries, the marriage has been arranged between the bridegroom and the father of the bride. And the bridegroom has paid a certain amount of money for the virgin daughter of the father. And a marriage contract signed. That contract is called a *ketubah*. It is a marriage contract whereby the obligations of a husband towards his wife are specified. This marriage contract has been in use in Judaism since the 1st century BCE.

This contract stipulates four times that the bridegroom must pay such and such an amount to the father for his virgin daughter. On their wedding night, the marriage is consummated on a special sheet. The next morning, this sheet is hung outside the tent or house with blood on it to show all that she had been, indeed, a virgin. That sheet is known from *Deuteronomy* 22:15 ff. as the "tokens of her virginity" and it stays with her for the rest of her life. If at any time her husband might accuse her of not being a virgin on their wedding night, the "tokens of her virginity" will be brought forth and displayed for all to see, and her husband can never divorce her from that moment for any reason. However, if it could be proven that she was, indeed, not a virgin on her wedding night, then the *ketubah* will be deemed to have been falsified and she may be put away with no dowry.

What Jesus is saying here is that there is no reason a man should put away his wife unless the marriage contract has been falsified. Should he put her away for no legal reason and she remarry, he has caused her to commit adultery because he has illegally put her away. And there were, in fact, legal reasons whereby a man might put away his wife and vice versa, although these are not being taken into consideration in *Matthew* 19:9. If, however, the man has been married to a woman whose conduct has given rise to a scandal, the husband is entitled to divorce her without paying the amount prescribed in the *ketubah*. Those who have their marriage dissolved without receiving what would otherwise be due them are:

1. Women who transgress Jewish law by going into public with their heads uncovered. At marriage, the bride covers her head and it is considered immodest for her to expose it.
2. Women who weave cloth in the streets or converse with men.
3. Women who curse the children of her husband in his presence.
4. Women who talk so loudly in the house that neighbors can hear what she says (*Ketubah* 7:6).

The woman also had grounds for divorce.

1. If her husband becomes repugnant to her either through loathsome illness or repugnant work.
2. Should blemishes appear in a man, the court does not compel him to divorce his wife. Rabbi Gamaliel contended that this is true of minor blemishes but that in the case of serious blemishes he is compelled to give her a divorce. The implication is of course that the serious blemishes would render him incapable of performing his conjugal duties.
3. If he was smitten with leprosy or developed a pedunculated tumor of the nasal membranes which would cause him to snore inordinately.

4. Or if he is a gatherer of dog dung or a copper smelter or a tanner. Whether these conditions existed before marriage or arose after marriage. Rabbi Maier declares with reference to all that even if the husband made an agreement with her, she is entitled to plead, "I thought I could endure it, but now I see I cannot."

Now, again, unless you understand all this, there is a lot you are going to miss in reading the *New Testament.* Why would anyone be a gatherer of dog dung? That's easy when you know that dog dung was used in tanning hides, a smelly business, indeed!

The profession of a tanner was justification for divorce. Why? Because the substances used in tanning were so noxious that the tannery was usually situated on the far, downwind side of the village or town.

In *Acts* 9 -10, Peter visits the city of Lydda. A disciple named Dorcas has died and so the disciples in Joppa sent for Peter asking him to come to Joppa without delay. When he arrives in Joppa, where do the disciples house him?...Uncomfortably in the house of Simon the tanner. It is no wonder, then, that Peter is up on the housetop when messengers arrive from Caesarea to ask him to come assist them.

Another engaging passage easily misunderstood without knowledge of *Mishnah* is the admonition of Paul in *1 Corinthians* 7:5 addressing the husband and wife relationship: "Do not cheat each other of normal sexual intercourse, unless of course you both decide to abstain temporarily to make special opportunity for fasting and prayer. But afterwards you should resume relations as before..." (*1 Corinthians* 7:5). Notice that the maximum length of time a couple could abstain from sexual intercourse was two weeks!

In *Ketubah* 5 and 6, if a man vows he will not have intercourse with his wife, the School of Shammai allowed him two weeks, but the School of Hillel only one week. If, by the end of that period, he does not annul his vow and resume intercourse, he is compelled to divorce his wife. A woman may also free herself from a distasteful marriage by vowing to withhold herself from her husband.

Despite the ease with which a union could be dissolved, the evidence does not suggest that it was abused. The high ideal of married life, enjoined and practiced during the time of the *Mishnah* and the *Talmud*, had raised the standard of Jewish marriage to a lofty level.

## CHAPTER 9
# HOMOSEXUALITY

References to homosexuality in Jewish literature are rare, which is interesting in view of the fact that the ancient Greeks accepted it as natural. In *The Symposium*, for example, Plato depicts love between two men as noble. Indeed, as more so than love between a man and a woman! Moreover, social researchers have ascertained that 64 percent of primitive societies accepted homosexuality within the framework of normalcy.

Three reasons are offered in Jewish Law for prohibition of homosexual marriage. First, it was considered a perversion of the natural endowments of humankind. The Creator clearly designed male and female genitalia to complement each other. Sigmund Freud once said, "Anatomy is destiny."[26]

Second, homosexuality frustrates the primary purpose of procreation. And, the primary commandment of Jewish law is, of course, to be fruitful and multiply.

Third, in theory at least, homosexuality threatens the survival of the human species and so of the Jewish people.

However, although the act of homosexuality is technically prohibited, not all practicing homosexuals should be arbitrarily lumped together. The response to each must be appropriate to his or her motives.

According to Maurice Lamm in his book *The Jewish Way in Love and Marriage*, six categories of homosexuality present themselves:[27]

1. Genuine homosexuality, that is purely biological, i.e., the person is simply born that way.
2. Transitory homosexual behavior, which occurs among adolescents who would prefer heterosexual experiences but are denied such for a number of reasons.
3. Situational homosexual experiences characteristic of prisoners, soldiers, others who are heterosexual but denied access to women for long periods of time.
4. Transitory and/or opportunistic sexual behavior – that of delinquent young men who permit themselves to be used by pederasts for money or other favors.
5. Those who experience their condition out of duress or uncontrollable passion and who transform their homosexuality into an ideology, such as the gay militants.
6. The notion that one must experience all sexual pleasures whether or not one feels inclined to them because they feel they must try everything at least once in their lives.

The subject of homosexuality is much more complicated than what appears on the surface. In a recent article published online, the author states that homosexuality is a core issue for the Christian faith. He states that "in all of the *Bible*, both the *Old Testament* and *New Testament*, homosexual practice is forbidden and viewed as sin. He continues to discuss that human creation as male and female is in some sense a reflection of the unity and diversity of the Holy Trinity.

When the tri-personal God creates, gendered human kind is a key result. Gendered human creation in the image of God is a core matter of human identity. Clearly, it establishes a biblical norm for persons, families, societies and culture. The consistent teachings of scripture regarding sexual ethics, both *hetero* and *homo*, thus fit naturally and logically into the coherence into the biblically revealed plan of salvation. The Internet author concludes that biblical fidelity requires viewing homosexual practice as sinful and a violation of God's law, and also requires unqualified compassion and understanding toward homosexual persons in the spirit of Jesus and led by the power of the Holy Spirit."[28]

*Really?* Let's see, for a moment, if we can't focus on a few basic facts and refrain from pious pontification.

True, the *Bible* states in *Genesis* 1:26-27 that God created man in his own image and in his own likeness. Certainly, this cannot mean a physical being since the *Bible* states that God is a spirit. (*John* 4:24) Without going into a lengthy dissertation on the subject, we might say that man's creation in the image and likeness of God refers to his spiritual dimension and not the physical.

In the physical dimension, we are simply born whatever we are, whether it be male, or female; or whether it be hermaphroditic; or whether one might be born with questionable gender. One may be born homosexual, heterosexual, or asexual. It ultimately depends upon your draw from the chromosomal lottery.

No one can simply *choose* to be born male or female or whatever. We don't choose to be born what we are. We simply are. We are male, female, questionable gender, hermaphroditic, homosexual, heterosexual, asexual, whatever. It is simply a matter of genetics. We didn't choose to be what we are, but as a "human being," created in "God's image," we must learn to play the chromosomal cards we were dealt in the most responsible, moral, ethical and non-judgmental way that we can.

That imperative is not going to be easy for a lot of us especially when we have to live with the onus placed upon us by a religious fundamentalism that is quick to condemn and slow to understand. Truly, understanding is a must!

We must understand that literally hundreds of children are born every day with all kinds of abnormalities with which they are going to have to live the rest of their lives. Each one of us is a unique individual. No two people are exactly alike. Our responsibility is to understand the uniqueness in our fellow human and try to educate ourselves as best we can to respect differences and assist each other in this journey we call life to the best of our ability. It is certainly not going to help to automatically condemn or label one condition or another as "sin."

Recent studies have indicated that a high percentage of homosexuality is genetic. Some are just born that way. These studies have revealed a correlation between homosexual orientation and the inheritance of polymorphic markers on the X chromosome. The marker known as Xq28 indicated a confidence level of more than 99 percent that at least one type of male sexual orientation is genetically influenced.[29]

The debate over the cause of homosexuality has continued to rage with some studies suggesting that the cause is perhaps more biologic than it is genetic. Some studies have pointed to the hypothalamus while more recent studies continue to link the causative factor to the X chromosome. Although we have certainly not heard the final word on the subject, nonetheless, recent research suggests that male gayness is an inborn, unalterable and strongly genetically influenced trait.[30]

Remember...homosexuals, transsexuals, whatever the cause might be, are human beings with feelings, emotions, likes, dislikes, hopes and dreams just like any other individual. Whether one agrees with their journey or not is far from the issue; acceptance and understanding is everyone's issue.

In most instances, prejudice and misunderstanding are based on a lack of knowledge of the original biblical text and Jewish culture. For example, there will be those who read this chapter and will declare, "But the *Bible* says that homosexuality in addition to other sexual sins is an abomination." They will automatically condemn and will be quick to consign all who practice such to hell.

There are actually three words in Hebrew that are translated into English as "abomination." The principle one is *to-evah*. *To-evah* is the most important of the words and it has a variety of applications ranging from food prohibition to idolatry and magic as well as sexual offenses. These sexual offenses are those that are described in *Leviticus* 18:22 ff.[31] The word used in this reference from *Leviticus* is akin to the word used in *Romans* 1:26-27, and in *1 Corinthians* 6:8 ff.

As previously mentioned, in order to understand any particular passage in the biblical text, it is essential that one see it not only in its linguistic context but also in its historical and cultural context. The religious and cultural context of the Hebrew people in the 1st century was diametrically opposed to that of Corinth and Rome – two of the cities in which Paul lived and to which he wrote.

The name Corinth became a synonym for immorality. The reputation of Corinth was such that the word *Korinthiazesthai*, to live like a Corinthian, had become a part of the Greek language and meant to live with drunken and immoral debauchery.

There were numerous temples in Corinth dedicated to the various Gods; such as Apollo, Hermes, Venus-Fortuna, Isis, and Aphrodite, the goddess of love. Attached to these temples were priests and priestesses who were sacred prostitutes. In the evenings, they would spread out across the city plying their trade. Since it was located on the coast, it became popular with sailors from the ends of the earth, to such a degree that Corinth became a synonym for wealth and luxury as well as drunkenness and filth.

When reading Paul in either *Romans* or *Corinthians*, his words must be seen in context with the culture of the city as well as the practices of the people to the east. For example: When Paul says in *1 Timothy* 2, that the "women are to keep silent in the Church," he is not setting forth a commandment that is to be generally practiced in the worship services, although it has frequently been interpreted as such. He is simply referring to the fact that in the Hellenistic world it was a common practice for the temple prostitute to assume a dominant role that they attempted to carry over into the early services of worship. However, it has been recently discovered and verified with inscriptional evidence that women functioned in the synagogue as well as in the Christian Churches in every capacity or function in which men served.

Paul's admonition was, therefore, directed to a certain group of individuals in a cultural context that was considered inappropriate and unseemly to those in the community of God. More specific information on this can be found in *Women Leaders in the Ancient Synagogue* by Bernadette Brooten.

Almost the entire chapter of *Leviticus* 18 deals with forbidden relationships. Few understand that these passages are directed specifically toward incest and other forbidden relationships. In *Leviticus* 18:22 when it speaks of homosexuality, it specifies that homosexuality is forbidden with one's father or uncle, just as the entire chapter is directed towards incestuous relationships. When Paul makes reference to this in *1 Corinthians* and in *Romans* that "homosexuality is an abomination" – it is referencing incestuous homosexuality in *Leviticus* 18.

When we read in *Leviticus* 18:3, "therefore you shall keep my charge that you do not any of the abominable customs which were done before you," it refers to the Canaanites and Amorites whose hallmark was the public display of sex – "*the abominable practice* of the nations."[32]

The point in this regard is that the alchemy of the cultic experience in ancient Canaan was public fornication and the orgies of the fertility cult with their temple prostitutes. The *Talmud* says, "There is no one so loathsome as one who walks naked in the street."

All of this is not to say that everything was legitimate and that there were no constraints upon sexual adventurism. The admonitions given herein were to assist in avoiding illicit sexual relationships.

Judaism would consider the difference between the various categories of homosexuality. Although any given act of homosexuality would be considered a *to-evah* or an abomination, it is necessary to distinguish between the act itself and the person who perpetrates the act. At one end of the spectrum would be those who are genuinely genetically disposed to homosexuality; whereas, opportunistic homosexuality, ideological homosexuality and transitory adult homosexuality would be at the other end of the spectrum. In other words, it is not only important but legitimate to distinguish between the act itself and the motivation driving the act. As Lamm points out (*The Jewish Way in Love and Marriage*, 70), "the objective crime remains a *maaseh averah* (violative action), whereas the person who transgresses it is considered innocent on the grounds of duress (Hebrew *ones*)." In other words, the response to the homosexual must contain a number of ingredients: knowledge of current research in the subject, intelligence, understanding and compassion.

What about female homosexuality? Female homosexuality or lesbianism is not mentioned in the *Bible*. It is discussed in rabbinic literature and, although the prohibition of male homosexuality is extended to the female, the penalty is not. It is not considered a specifically sexual sin. Rather, only an *issur*, a minor moral offense.

Maimonides classified it as a *peritzut* or promiscuity rather than a *zenut*, a violation of the sexual prohibition. He did so because in lesbianism there is no genital intercourse and so, no destruction of the seed of Abraham. Thus it was not considered a perversion of God's intent.

Perhaps there were other reasons as well. The positive command to be fruitful and multiply does not apply to the female. Also, many women were attached to the harem of a single man, and so, turned to other women. Realizing we are all sexual beings, Jewish law is much more considerate of the sexual needs of the female. Therefore, there is no biblical proscription of lesbianism.

Sexual relations are seen not merely as a means for perpetuating the species but as a part of the human personality. It is not only a channel of life but a channel of love.

Judaism teaches that God did not plan the reproductive organs as strictly mechanical means for the production of new life: God constructed the human being to appreciate the physical and soulful ecstasy of the sexual act. Saadia Gaon noted that his view and the view of some of his contemporaries was that "sexual intercourse holds the most remarkable of pleasures. It increases the soul's gladness and gaiety; it drives gloomy thoughts from the mind and serves as an antidote to melancholy. And, there cannot be anything reprehensible about the sex act since God's holy men in the *Bible* engaged in it with his approval."[33]

Today there is much discussion on the subject of homosexual marriage. In reality, homosexual "marriage" would be a fallacy in concept within the parameters of ancient religious law. The term "marriage" began as a religious concept and the religious definition of marriage is traditionally as a covenant between a man and a woman.

It may be healthy for society as a whole to take the entire concept of marriage out of a religious context and focus simply on a civil union or a contract that would be performed and endorsed by the State as opposed to the Church. Parity of rights, privileges and responsibilities would thus be assured, as with any traditional marriage.

A considered understanding that the legalization of same sex unions in modern times is a Civil Rights issue rather than an issue of religion, will accelerate the process of equality. Remember, our country was built on the concept of the separation of Church and State, an idea that should certainly be sufficient to allow homosexuals of every ilk to enjoy all of the rights, privileges and responsibilities automatically provided to those engaged in a religiously endorsed union.

It is important to note that the Diagnostic and Statistical Manual of Mental Disorders (or DMS-5) of 2013 no longer lists homosexuality as a psychological problem that can be treated. The American Psychological Association has not listed homosexuality as a problem that can be treated since 1973.

## CHAPTER 10
# TRANSSEXUALISM

Any discussion of human sexuality naturally leads us to a consideration of transsexuality. Transsexuality is much more common than one might suppose and deserves both considerable discussion and consideration. Transsexuality is distinct and separate from both homosexuality and transvestism.

Transvestism, also called cross-dressing, simply indicates the desire of a person of one sex to be clothed in garments of a person of the opposite sex. To be honest, although this is a rather common fetish, we sex educators or therapists know neither the cause nor any satisfactory treatment of it. It is interesting to note that most cross-dressers are not gay, and fit into society perfectly in every other way.

Transsexualism is a completely different condition. Many more individuals experience this condition than what you might suppose.

The latest thinking is that a person is not actually a *transgender*, insofar as they believe that they should have been the opposite gender from the start. The terms becoming popular is *transitioning* or *Gender Reassignment*, as the person who has undergone successful psychiatric counseling as well as a medical regimen to prepare them for their *transition* into the gender which they believe they were originally intended to be. They insist that they have always known that something was "not right", even in early childhood.

The reason, whether identifying as transgender or transitioning, is at once subtle and obvious. Every fetus starts out as a female. It is not until the ninth week that the gonads signal the fetal brain to start producing the male hormone, testosterone. From that time onward, the production of testosterone sends the fetus on its path toward maleness.

Unfortunately, many things can go wrong and often do: the natural means the female body has of ridding itself of a foreign substance, for example. All eggs and one in two sperm have an X chromosome, which carries the female factor. The other sperm have a Y chromosome, carrying the male factor. If a sperm with an X chromosome fertilizes an egg, the resulting child will have two X chromosomes and the offspring will be female. But, if fertilization is by a sperm with a Y chromosome, the child will have one X and one Y chromosome and be male.

Errors in the reassortment and recombination of chromosomes during sex-cell formation result in any number of sex abnormalities. For example, a XXX combination may result in a normal looking but possibly infertile female. And an XYY combination may result in a male with normal sex organs but perhaps other problems. Also a combination such as XXY or XXXYY may produce males whose sex organs remain immature and who may develop female secondary sexual characteristics.

Because the Y chromosome is a foreign substance in the female body, miscarriage is the natural means the female body has in ridding itself of the foreign substance. Thus approximately 80% of miscarriages are male. However, the more male children that the woman has, the more acclimated her body becomes to the Y chromosome. Accordingly, we now know that the third male child born to a mother is more likely to manifest feminine characteristics or become homosexual.

Because so many things can go wrong and often do, the child may be born with underdeveloped genitals resulting in questionable gender. Unfortunately, it has too often been the practice of the attending physician, without consulting the parents, simply to rearrange the genitals as he/she thinks they should be without doing a simple chromosomal test to find out if the child has XX or XY chromosomes – or some other combination.

As a result, many children who grow into puberty and adolescence feel trapped in the wrong body. That is, a male trapped in a female body or vice versa. These are not homosexuals. Rather, they are caught in a sex-role inversion, a complex situation in which one believes that he or she has been given the body of the wrong sex.

Transsexuals spend most of their life hating their body, which they consider unnatural. They may spend most of their life desiring a physical change of sex to align them with their true gender identity. Although we find, from time to time, female-to-male transsexuals, transsexualism occurs mainly in men. The male transsexual usually has normal male genitals and is physically capable of both having intercourse and fathering children. I have personally had cases of transsexuals who have fathered children. One had five and another three when they finally broke down and could no longer deny their true sexuality.

Another recently brought to light is of a transgendered male, a father of three, now legally a female, who remains legally and happily married in a State which passed a

Constitutional Amendment banning same-sex marriage! That's right, a genuine Mr. Mom!

Often, they come to hate their sex organs so intensely that they may castrate themselves or commit suicide. Typically, the male transsexual wants to be a woman and, as a woman, to have a heterosexual relationship with a man. Although he may obtain some relief from dressing as a woman, he is mainly concerned with a surgical sex change. Such operations have been greatly refined in the last 30 years with hundreds being performed in the United States annually.

However, before a male-to-female sex change operation can take place, the candidate must satisfy certain preconditions:

1. First, receive psychiatric counseling.
2. Second, take female hormones.
3. Third, living full-time as a female.
4. Fourth, receive breast augmentation.

After the candidate has satisfied these four preconditions, the operation takes place in which the genitals are remodeled. It is often quite difficult to ascertain that such has ever taken place.

Transsexualism is a condition that is even more complicated than homosexuality. Early detection and adequate counseling can only offer marginal help. Even though the transsexual may expect all of their problems and/or fears to be conquered after sexual realignment has taken place, such is frequently not the case. They often continue to have problems, mental and physical as well as social and societal, of one kind or another that must be addressed. Probably more so than with other individuals continued therapy and/or counseling with a qualified therapist would be most beneficial. One should not think that simply because they have gone through gender realignment that all of their problems are suddenly going to disappear. In most instances, such is not the case. Do not and I repeat, do not fail to continue with counseling and/or therapy until those said problems and/or fears are alleviated.

This gender-identity disorder is much more common than one might expect. All individuals of good will would do well to go online and look at a number of Web sites that are devoted to the subject of transsexualism.

Perhaps more than anything else, parents of transsexual children need to be both understanding and accommodating in helping their offspring to discover their true identity and be able to live a completely normal and fruitful life.

Just as with homosexuality, the DMS-5 of 2013 states that being transgender is no longer considered a mental disorder.

## CHAPTER 11
## MASTURBATION

Even though we have dealt at some length with the long-winded bombast of old Professor O.S. Fowler on masturbation, our knowledge of what the *Bible* teaches about this topic requires additional commentary.

There has long been a heavy sense of sin and shame associated with masturbation, both male and female. Traditionally, many generations ago, Jewish law declared masturbation by men as a wrongful act relative to an incident related to the Jewish subject of Levirate law. Jewish law taught that if a man died without offspring, his oldest brother was to have intercourse with the widow so that the offspring could legally become heir of the deceased brother.

Here is a summary of the story:

> Er, son of Judah died. Judah then requested that Onan have sexual intercourse and impregnate Tamar, Er's widow. Onan had sex with Tamar, but performed *coitus interruptus*, spilling his seed on

the ground so there would not be any offspring he could not claim as his own. *Genesis* 38: 8-9 states that God was displeased and that Onan was punished for his disobedience.

Even today, *coitus interruptus* is often identified with onanism and onanism with masturbation. It is important to emphasize that masturbation is not considered synonymous with onanism.

Women masturbate but Jewish sources offer little or no discussion on the subject of female masturbation. The focus is on the male for two reasons. Lesbianism is not a violation of the first positive commandment to be fruitful and multiply. That commandment is only upon men. Second, in female masturbation, there is obviously no emission of sperm or the seed of Abraham as it is with the male. Although the practice was frowned upon, legal writers had difficulty in discussing any biblical basis for their abhorrence. No less an authority than Maimonides claimed it could not be punishable by any court because there was no explicit negative commandment forbidding it.

Judaism offers three perspectives on the subject of masturbation: Orthodox, Conservative, and Reformed/Progressive. Today many Orthodox Jews retain the more conservative beliefs and prohibitions. But the Conservative and the Reformed and/or Progressive Jews do not. Their more liberal view derives from increased medical knowledge as well as the realities of our modern world. Poor old Professor Fowler, that is, has been proven terribly wrong. In view of the fact that more and more of our young men and women are waiting longer to marry, realistically speaking, the choices for teenagers and people in their 20's and early 30's are either to masturbate or to engage in non-marital sex.

For many people, especially religious fundamentalists, masturbation is a taboo topic. The many harmful myths about masturbation may lead to guilt, shame and fear. We need to get one thing straight: masturbation is a natural and a common activity for both men and women. Studies indicate that 7 out of 10 adult men and more than 5 out of 10 adult women masturbate. It is common for children and teens. However, people may begin masturbating at most any time in their lives as they begin to grow and explore their changing bodies. Because it feels good, children usually begin masturbating long before puberty. It is important for children to learn that it is normal and will not hurt their bodies. Rather, it can be good for both mental and physical health and is also one of the best ways to learn about one's sexuality.

Learning what feels good to you can often increase your chances of sexual pleasure with your sex partner. When you know what you like, what feels good, your confidence and comfort level increase and it is easier to let your partner know what you like. It can frequently help people know how they like to be touched and stimulated sexually. It can improve relationships and sexual satisfaction and is often used to provide treatment for sexual dysfunction.

Many people, because of their religious upbringing, feel shame or guilt about masturbating. Approximately 50 percent of both men and women do feel guilty. If you feel guilty or worry, you need to ask yourself, "Does masturbation interfere with my daily functions?" If it interferes or gets in the way of your job, your responsibilities or your social life, you may need to consult with a therapist. One basic problem that we do see is when men masturbate so frequently that it can negatively affect their ability to engage in a satisfying relationship with their female partner and/or achieve orgasm without some form of manual stimulation. In such cases, you may need to discuss your situation with a sex educator or therapist.

One final word on the subject: although there was a period from the late 18$^{th}$ to the early 20$^{th}$ century when masturbation was subject to all kinds of medical and religious censure, it is considered, in most circles, a normal part of a healthy sexual life today.

## CHAPTER 12
## PREMARITAL SEX

Before we conclude our study I want to add a word or two about sex outside marriage. Of all of the questions that I get, the most frequent has to do with sex outside of marriage. The Jewish or biblical position on sexual activity outside marriage is complex. In general, the *Torah* does not outlaw it as it does some specific acts in *Leviticus* 20 ff. And, the *Torah* sees the child born of sexual activity outside of marriage as entirely legitimate. Since marital sex is considered *Kiddushin*, or holiness, most Jewish authorities disapprove of sex without marriage simply because it does not adequately fit the description of *Kiddushin*.

What about a long-term committed sexual relationship in which two people are exclusive partners? As earlier mentioned, the *Torah* does not outlaw such activity and both rabbinic and traditional sources have been quite lenient in the area. For example, Nachmanides permitted sex with an unmarried woman who was not involved with another man. However, such activity is not without legal complications in that the *Torah* prohibits sex, marital or otherwise, between a man and a woman who is menstruating.

The *Torah* does sanction one type of non-marital sexual activity – concubinage. A concubine is a woman who, though involved exclusively with one man, does not receive the legal benefits of marriage. As we have seen previously, in biblical times concubines were kept in addition to a wife or wives.

In recent times, many Jewish authorities have dismissed the validity of concubinage. But, some more liberal authorities are, once again, exploring this viability. They point out the need to develop a new sexual ethic to address the reality of adult sexual relationships. Some have even suggested altering our expectation of marriage to make it easy for sexually active people from puberty on to engage in sexual activities without fear of reprisal by both religious and secular authorities.

Although most continue to stress the ideal of marriage, many acknowledge that what is being said by religious authorities is, again, not consistent with what is actually happening in our contemporary society. Therefore, we should stress the need for up-to-date sex education in our public schools beginning as early as the fifth or sixth grades.

In summation, sexual relations outside of marriage may be considered improper but ultimately have no legal impact on one's future marriage. Religious authorities, nonetheless, continue to stress the importance of modesty, fidelity, health, and safety, even in non-marital relationships.

## CHAPTER 13
# CONCLUSIONS AND QUESTIONS

Today there are many voices and individuals out there proclaiming to be authorities on various subjects relating to the *Bible*. There are so many voices that a person can be easily confused or deceived, unable to discern fact from fiction and truth from error. Unfortunately, many of these self-proclaimed authorities have vast audiences on TV or through publications; they are reaching tens of thousands of people. Today, more than any other time in history, there is a greater number of people from diverse backgrounds who are searching for truth in their lives and don't know where to turn.

I am going to make a suggestion that has been our ministry's motto for several years now: "Question the Answers." Don't believe everything that you hear. Don't believe everything that you read, including what is written here. Check the sources. Check the supposed authorities. Even if a person calls himself or herself Doctor this or Doctor that, it doesn't necessarily mean that they have a legitimately earned Doctorate degree. Many, in fact, are either honorary or may have been purchased from a diploma mill. Be sure to ask *what are the credentials that give them the authority to speak on a particular subject?*

Today, more than ever, when people talk about what the *Bible* says or doesn't say, the first question that one should ask is, *Does the speaker have knowledge of the original biblical languages? (Hebrew/Greek.) Are they fluent and/or capable of working with the original texts? Are they knowledgeable in the historical and cultural background that gave birth to this material?*

This is essential because the historical and cultural context of the timeframe in which the material was written (two-to-three millennia ago) was quite different than what is being taught today.

This may be difficult but there is one simple question to ask that can assist in determining truth from error, fact from fiction. That question is: "When this teaching is practically applied in my life, does it bring me into bondage or does it set me free?"

If it brings you into bondage to a doctrine, a denomination or an individual, chances are it is not from God. The biblical text proclaims, "Where the Spirit of the Lord is, there is liberty." (*2 Corinthians* 3:17) Liberty, however, does not mean license. Liberty is not a license to do what you want but it is a license to do what you ought.

The great German philosopher, Immanuel Kant (ca 1781) wrote, "Dare to know! Have the courage to use your own intelligence!" Kant's admonition is my challenge to you and my motivation for finally undertaking this work.

To share your thoughts or ask a question, please visit us online at www.biblescholars.org.

# APPENDIX I

## FEMALE REPRODUCTIVE SYSTEM

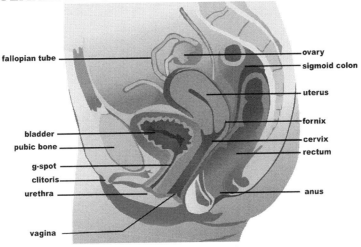

© *Jelena Zaric / Fotolia*

The female reproductive system consists of two ovaries, two fallopian tubes, the uterus, the cervix, and the vagina.

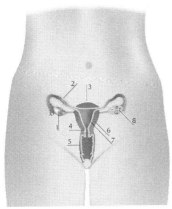

1. Ovary
2. Fallopian tube
3. Uterus
4. Cervix
5. Vagina
6. Myometrium
7. Endometrial (uterine) lining
8. Eggs developing inside ovary

© *Elena Baryshkina / Fotolia*

# APPENDIX II

## MALE REPRODUCTIVE SYSTEM

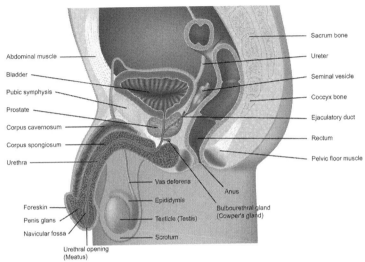

© *Peter Junaidy / Fotolia*

Organs of the male reproductive system include the penis, testes, and epididymis. Several ducts and glands are also part of the system. Do you know the reproductive functions of any of these structures? Visit http://bitly.com/male-reproductive-system.

# ENDNOTES

[1] *Ancient Near Eastern Texts Relating to the Old Testament*, edited by James B. Pritchard, Princeton University Press, New Jersey, 1969, 644-645.
[2] Herodotus, *The Histories*, Penguin Books, New York, 1954, 92.
[3] Date hookup.com, "Life of a Woman in Ancient Greece and Rome", http://www.datehookup.com/content-the-life-of-a-woman-in-ancient-greece-and-rome.htm, (accessed October 8, 2013).
[4] D.S. Bailey, *Sexual Relations in Christian Thought*, Harper, New York, 1959, 19-20.
[5] Gershom Scholem, *Major Trends in Jewish Mysticism*, Schocken, New York, 1974, 13.
[6] Bailey, 55.
[7] David M. Feldman, *Marital Relations, Birth Control and Abortion in Jewish Law*, Schocken, New York, 1974, 86-87.

[8] Brown-Driver-Briggs, *Hebrew and English Lexicon*, Hendrickson, Massachusetts, 1979, 326 #2530.
[9] Bailey, 135-36.
[10] Alexander Hislop, *The Two Babylons*, orig. pub. 1919, Loizeaux Brothers, New Jersey, 1959, Chapter 6, Section 2.
[11] O. S. Fowler, *phrenology and physiology, Creative and Sexual Science: Manhood, Womanhood and their Mutual Interrelations. Love, Its Laws, Powers, etc., Selection or Mutual Adaptation, Courtship, Married life and Perfect Children*, National Publishing Co., Philadelphia, Chicago and St. Louis, 1870, 873-4.
[12] David Flusser, *Jewish Sources in Early Christianity*, Adama Books, New York, 1987, 11-12.
[13] Bailey, 100-101.
[14] Raphael Patai, *Family, Love and the Bible*, MacGibbon & Kee, London, 1960, 149.
[15] Feldman, 74.
[16] Feldman, 99.
[17] Feldman, 100.
[18] Wouk, Herman, *This is My God*, (Dell paperback edition., 1988), 125.
[19] Feldman, 155-156.
[20] Feldman, 169.
[21] Dictionary.com, *American Heritage Dictionary of the English Language, 4th edition*, Houghton Mifflin Co., Life definition, http://dictionary.reference.com/browse/life, (accessed October 8, 2013).
[22] Rabbi Hayim Halevy Donin, *To be a Jew*, Basic Books, New York, 1972, 141.
[23] Feldman, 291.
[24] Raymond J. Lawrence, Jr., *The Poisoning of Eros: Sexual Values in Conflict*, Augustine Moore Press, New York, 1989, 256-7.
[25] Lawrence, 257.

[26] *Sigmund Freud: Collected Writings*, (1924), vol. 5, p. 210, Source: Oxford Dictionary of Quotations.
[27] Maurice Lamm, *The Jewish Way in Love and Marriage*, Harper & Row Publishers, San Francisco, CA., 1982, 69-70.
[28] Seedbed.com, "Is Homosexuality a Core Issue?", Howard Snyder, posted in Bible and Theology, 2012, http://seedbed.com/feed/is-homosexuality-a-core-issue, (accessed October 8, 2013).
[29] *Science*, "A Linkage Between DNA Markers on the X Chromosome in Male Sexual Orientation", The American Association for the Advancement of Science, 16 July 1993, Vol. 261, no. 5119, 321-327.
[30] Huffingtonpost.com, "Male Homosexuality Study: Gay Men Have Evolutionary Benefit For Their Families, New Research Suggests", Natalie Wolcover, June 14, 2012, http://www.huffingtonpost.com/2012/06/12/why-are-there-gay-men_n_1590501.html, (accessed October 8, 2013).
[31] *Encyclopedia Judaica*, Vol. 5, 781 and 782.
[32] Lamm, 139.
[33] Lamm, 135.

# BIBLIOGRAPHY

Cohen, Abraham, *Every Man's Talmud: The Major Teachings of the Rabbinic Sages*, Schocken, New York, first edition 1887, copyright 1995.

Feldman, David M., *Marital Relations, Birth Control, and Abortion in Jewish Law*, Schocken, New York, 1987.

Flusser, David, (Prof), *Jewish Sources in Early Christianity*, Mod Books, New York, 1989.

Fowler, O. S. Professor, *Creative and Sexual Science: Manhood, Womanhood and their Mutual Interrelations. Love, Its Laws, Powers, etc., Selection or Mutual Adaptation, Courtship, Married life and Perfect Children*, National Publishing Co., Philadelphia, Chicago and St. Louis, 1870.

Hawton, Keith, *Sex Therapy: A Practical Guide*, Oxford University Press, Toronto, New York, 1985.

HeChasid, Rabbi Yehudah, *Sefer Chasidim: The Book of the Pious*, from the late 12th century, Condensed,

Translated and Annotated by Avraham Yaakov Finkel, Jason Aronson, New Jersey, 1996.

Inkeles, Gordon and Todris, Murray, *The Art of Sensual Massage*, with photographs by Robert Footherap, Simon & Schuster, 1972. (Note: This book might assist a couple in getting acquainted and exploring one another's bodies.)

Johns, Catherine, *Sex or Symbol? Erotic Images of Greece and Rome*, Routledge, London, England, 1999.

Lamm, Maurice, *The Jewish Way in Love and Marriage*, Jonathan David Co., Inc, New York., 2008.

Lawrence, Raymond J., Jr., *The Poisoning of Eros: Sexual Values in Conflict*, Augustine Moore Press, New York, 1989.

Naham, Rabbi Moses Ben (Nachmanides), *Iggeret ha-Kodesh – The Holy Epistle*, from the late 12th century.

Rankin, Lissa, M.D., and Northrup Christiane, M.D., (introduction), *What's Up Down There?: Questions You'd Only Ask Your Gynecologist If She Was Your Best Friend*, St. Martin's Press, New York, 2010.

Scholem, Gershom, *Major Trends in Jewish Mysticism*, Schocken, New York, 1995.

Tannahill, Reay, *Sex in History*, Scarborough House Publishers, Maryland, 1992.

The Diagram Group, *Sex: A User's Manual*, Berkley, New York, 1985.

Wincze, John P. and Carey, Michael P., *Sexual Dysfunction, Second Edition: A Guide for Assessment and Treatment*, The Guilford Press, New York, 2001.

Wouk, Herman, *This is My God*, Little Brown and Company, New York, 1992.

---------, *Reader's Digest ABCs of the Human Boy, A Family Answer Book*, The Reader's Digest Assn., 1987.

---------, *The Mishnah: Order Nezikin*.

---------, *The Mishnah: Order Nashim*.

# GLOSSARY OF TERMS

**Abortion** – n. – termination of pregnancy by removal or expulsion, from the uterus, of a fetus or embryo prior to viability

**Abstemious** – adj. – characterized by abstinence or moderation

**Abstinence** – n. – voluntary restraint from indulging in bodily activities widely known to give pleasure

**Adductor magnus** – n. – a large triangular muscle, situated on the medial side of the thigh

**Adulterer** – n. – a married man who has had sex with a person other than his wife

**Adulteress** – n. – a married woman who has had sex with a person other than her husband

**Adultery** – n. – sexual infidelity to one's spouse, a form of extramarital sex

**Allegory** – n. – A story, poem, or picture that can be interpreted to reveal a hidden meaning, typically a moral or political one

**Anatomical** – adj. – Relating to the structure of an organism

**Androgyny** – n. – ambiguous sexual identity; neither clearly masculine nor clearly feminine in appearance

**Annul** – v. – declare invalid

**Aphrodisiac** – n. – a food, drug, potion, or other agent that arouses sexual desire

**Aquinas, Thomas** – name – (1225-1274), a 13$^{th}$ century Italian Dominican priest of the Roman Catholic Church, and an immensely influential philosopher and theologian in the tradition of scholasticism; also known as Doctor Angelicus ([the] Angelic Doctor)

**Arnobius** – name – **Arnobius of Sicca** (died c. 330), an Early Christian apologist

**Ascetic** – n. – one who, for religious reasons, dedicates his or her life contemplative ideals and practices, extreme self-denial, or self-mortification; one who leads an austerely simple life, especially abstaining from the normal pleasures of life

**Ataraxia** – n. – a state of freedom from emotional disturbance and anxiety; calmness or peace of mind; emotional tranquility

**Augustine** – name – "St. Augustine of Hippo," often simply "Augustine" (354-430 CE): *rhetor*, Christian Neoplatonist, North African Bishop, Doctor of the Roman Catholic Church; a Latin philosopher and theologian from Roman Africa whose writings were very influential in the development of Western Christianity

**'Avon** or **'avone** – Hebrew n. – (pronounced aw-vone') crookedness or to be bent, perversity, depravity, iniquity, guilt – found 229 times in the biblical text and often mistakenly translated as "sin" in the English *Bible*

**BCE** – acronym – before the Common or Current Era, BC

**Bacchanalia** – n. – ancient Roman festival in honor of Bacchus, god of wine and revelry

**Bailey, D. S.** – name – (1910-1984) **Derrick Sherwin Bailey**; A Christian theologian, whose writings helped the Church of England respond to theological issue of homosexuality, to homosexuals themselves, to the laws of England and provided important conceptual guidelines for subsequent discussions about homosexuality, not only in the Church of England but throughout Christendom

***Baraita*** – Hebrew n. – literally "external", "outside"; designates a tradition in the Jewish oral law not incorporated in the *Mishnah*

**Biblical Hebrew** – n. – also called **Classical Hebrew**, the archaic form of the Hebrew language, a Canaanite Semitic language spoken in the area known as Canaan between the Jordan River and the Mediterranean Sea. Biblical Hebrew is attested from about the 10$^{th}$ century BCE, and continued through the Second Temple period (ending in 70 CE)

**Brutish** – adj. – crude in feeling or manner; rough; uncivilized

**C (c)** – n. – century

**CE** – acronym – Common Era (sometimes Current Era or Christian Era), traditionally identified with *Anno Domini* (abbreviated AD)

**Caldarium** – n. – hot and steamy bath, used in a Roman bath complex; heated by a hypocaust, an under floor heating system

***Chalitzah*** – Hebrew n. – (pronounced khah-LEE-tzah) the shoe-removal ceremony relieving a brother-in-law of his obligation to marry his widowed sister-in-law

**Chastity** – n. – virginity, celibacy

***Chet*** – Hebrew n. – (pronounced *khet*) offense; reference to an arrow which "missed the target." The archer is not "bad." Rather, he made a mistake – due to a lack of focus, concentration or skill; appears 459 times in the biblical text, often translated as "sin" in the English *Bible*

**Cicero** – name – (106 BCE-43 BCE) Roman consul, orator, and writer

**Circa (ca)** – Latin prep. – "around," i.e., approximately

***Circus Maximus*** – Latin n. – large circus; Ancient Rome's largest venue for public games, which could accommodate about 150,000 spectators; Originally established in Regal era (753-509 BCE) and utilized into the Imperial era (27 BCE to 565 CE)

**Clitoris** – n. – a part of the female anatomy; a sensitive external organ of the reproductive system in female mammals and some other animals that is capable of becoming erect; located above or in front of the urethra

**Coitus** – n. – Sexual intercourse, also known as copulation or coitus

***Coitus interruptus*** – Latin phrase – a.k.a. withdrawal or pull-out method of birth-control in which a man, during intercourse, withdraws his penis from a woman's vagina prior to ejaculation

**Concubine** – n. – Woman who cohabits with a man to whom she is not legally married

**Concupiscence** – n. – Strong sexual desire

**Condom** – n. – a flexible sheath, usually made of thin rubber or latex, designed to cover the penis during sexual intercourse for contraceptive purposes or as a means of preventing sexually transmitted diseases

**Conjugal** – adj. – pertaining to the marriage or relating to husband and wife

**Contraception** – n. – intentional prevention of conception or impregnation through use of various devices, agents, drugs, sexual practices, or surgical procedures

**Convent** – n. – A community of persons devoted to religious life under a superior

***Crura*** – plural of crus, – n. – Latin for "leg"; leg-shaped strands of the clitoris, within the vagina

**Cult prostitute** – n. – sacred prostitution, temple

prostitution, or religious prostitution that was a practice of worship in ancient times

**Cunnilingus** – n. – oral stimulation of the genitals; sexual activity in which the female genitalia are stimulated by the partner's lips and tongue

**Cybele** – name – a mother goddess of Rome at the center of a rather bloody Phrygian cult; sometimes known as *Magna Mater*, or "great goddess"

**Cynicism** – proper n. – denoting Greek philosophical sect flourishing in 3$^{rd}$ century BCE and featuring Diogenes' stress on asceticism

**D (d)** – abbreviation v. – died

**Deacon** – n. – a subordinate officer in a Christian church; a Roman Catholic, Anglican, or Eastern Orthodox cleric ranking next below a priest; one of the laymen elected by a church with congregational polity to serve in worship, in pastoral care, and on administrative committees

**Divorce** – n. – (dissolution of marriage) the final termination of a marital union, canceling the legal duties and responsibilities of marriage and dissolving the bonds of matrimony between the parties

**Douching** – v. – streaming water, often containing medicinal or cleansing agents, applied to a body part or cavity for hygienic or therapeutic purposes; sometimes used as a form of birth control

***Dyspareunia*** – Greek n. – painful sexual intercourse, arising from medical or psychological causes (The symptom is reported almost exclusively by women, although the problem can also occur in men.)

**Episiotomy** – n. – surgical incision of the perineum to enlarge the vaginal opening for obstetrical purposes during the birth process

***Epistle of Holiness*** (see *Iggeret Hakodesh*)

**Era of Enlightenment** – Phrase – An elite cultural

movement of intellectuals in 18th century Europe that stressed reason in order to reform society and advance knowledge. It opposed intolerance and abuses in Church and state. Originating ca 1650-1700, it was shaped mainly by Baruch Spinoza (1632-1677), John Locke (1632-1704), Pierre Bayle (1647-1706), Isaac Newton (1643-1727) and Voltaire (1694-1778).

**Eroticism** – n. – sexually suggestive symbolism and settings in art at large, especially film, sculpture, and painting

**Euphemism** – n. – substitution of a mild, indirect, or vague expression for one thought to be offensive, harsh, or blunt; example, "to pass away" is a euphemism for "to die."

**Felatio** – n. – a sexual activity in which the penis is stimulated by the partner's mouth

**"G-spot"** – n. – (named after Ernst Grafenberg, 1881-1957) in women, a mass of tissue located on the anterior vaginal wall at the pubic hairline. When directly stimulated, it elicits a sensation that leads to orgasm and frequently ejaculation.

**Golden mean** – n. – the "middle way" between two extremes; Chief expositor Aristotle (384-322) in his *Nicomachean Ethics* (ca 350 BCE) elaborated the "golden mean" is the middle way between two undesirable extremes, one of excess and the other of deficiency

*Gyne* – Greek n. – a bearer of children

*Halacha* – Hebrew n. – (pronounced ha-la-ka') Jewish Law, from the root *Halach* or *to walk*, the basic meaning of *halacha* is the way in which one is to walk

*Hamad* – Hebrew n. – lust in Hebrew – in a bad sense means inordinate, ungoverned, selfish desire; desire of an idolatrous tendency; desire that motivates the individual to possess the thing desired at any cost (also *chamad* – "covet," usually for evil purposes)

**Harmitu** – n. – one of a class of sacred prostitutes

found throughout the ancient Middle East, especially associated with a harem

**Hasidism** – n. – a Jewish mystical movement; emphasis on religious enthusiasm rather than on learning; strong in 18<sup>th</sup> century, weak today

**Hebraic Roots** – n. – contemporary movement that advocates the return and adherence to the 1<sup>st</sup> century faith of Jesus Christ by seeking a better understanding of the culture, history, and religio-political backdrop of that era which led to the core differences with both the Jewish, and later, Christian communities

**Hellenistic** – adj. – relating to postclassical Greek history and culture from the death of Alexander the Great (323 BCE) to the defeat of Antony and Cleopatra (30 BCE); relating to or in the style of the Greek art or architecture of this period

**Hermaphroditicism** – n. – human being with both male and female reproductive sex organs

**Herodotus** – name – Greek Historian (ca 485 BCE-ca 425 BCE) known as "the Father of History;" 5<sup>th</sup> century BCE Greek historian whose writings, chiefly concerning the Persian Wars, are the earliest known examples of narrative history

*Hetaerae* – Greek n. – Courtesans in Ancient Greece; roughly comparable to Japanese Geishas of today

**Hillel** – (see **School of Hillel**)

***Homo sapiens (H. sapiens)*** – Latin phrase – modern species of humans; archaic forms of *Homo sapiens* evolved around 300,000 years ago; all humans now living belong to the subspecies *Homo sapien sapiens*

**Homosexual** – n. – one sexually attracted only to members of same sex

**Homosexuality** – n. – Sexual orientation to persons of the same sex; Sexual activity with another of the same sex

**Horace** – name – **Quintus Horatius Flaccus** (65-8

BCE); Roman lyric poet; His *Odes and Satires* have exerted a major influence on English poetry

**Hugh of Pisa** – name – an Italian Classical canon lawyer (d. in 1210); most famous of all decretists; His major non-legal work is the *Magnae Derivationes* or *Liber derivationum*, dealing with etymologies, based on the earlier *Derivationes* of Osbernus of Gloucester

**Idiom** – n. – an expression whose meaning is not predictable from the usual meanings of its constituent elements; i.e., "kick the bucket"; a language, dialect, or style of speaking peculiar to a people

**Idiomatic** – adj. – peculiar to or characteristic of a particular language or dialect: idiomatic French

***Iggeret Hakodesh*** (*The Holy Epistle*) – Hebrew title – book written by Nahmanides on marriage, holiness, and sexual relations; the body is a work of God, thereby holy, as are normal sexual impulses of the body

**Infanticide** – n. – homicide of an infant, usually female; considered permissible in certain past societies; flourished especially in ancient Sparta

**IUCD** – n. – abbreviation for intrauterine contraceptive device; a birth control device, such as a plastic or metallic loop, ring, or spiral, that is inserted into the uterus to prevent implantation

**Intercourse** – n. – physical sexual contact between individuals that involves the genitalia of at least one person

**Ishtar** – Greek name – mythological goddess of the Babylonians and Assyrians; divinity of love, fertility, and war

***Ishtaritu*** – Greek n. – prostitutes who served the goddess Ishtar

**Isis** – name – a goddess in Ancient Egyptian religious beliefs, whose worship spread throughout the Greco-Roman world; worshipped as the ideal mother and wife as well as the patron of nature and magic

***Issur*** – Hebrew n. – a religious transgression rather than sin

**Jerome** – name – (c.t7-420) a Roman Christian priest, confessor, theologian and historian who became a Doctor of the Church; best known for his translation of the *Bible* into Latin (the *Vulgate*), his list of writings is extensive; recognized by the Catholic Church as a saint and Doctor of the Church

**Jesus** – Hebrew name – Jesus of Nazareth in 1$^{st}$ century Jerusalem is a teacher and prophet born in Bethlehem and active in Nazareth; his life and sermons recorded today in the *Synoptic Gospels* form the basis for Christianity, (circa 4 BCE-29 CE), also (see **School of Jesus**)

**Kegal exercises** – phrase – various exercises involving controlled contraction and release of the muscles at the base of the pelvis, used especially as treatment for urinary incontinence

***Ketubah*** – Hebrew n. – "document"; a special type of Jewish prenuptial agreement; considered an integral part of a traditional Jewish marriage; outlines the rights and responsibilities of the groom, in relation to the bride

***Kiddushin*** – Hebrew n. – the Hebrew word for sanctification or dedication, also called *erusin* (betrothal), the first of the two stages of the Jewish wedding process

**Lascivious** – Latin adj. – lustful, lecherous

***Lesammeah*** – Hebrew n. – cause to rejoice or be happy; requirement that a husband give joy to his wife in the manner of the *Mitzvah* of *Onah*

**Licentious** – adj. – adjective for license; lacking moral restraints, especially in sexual matters

**Lesbos (Island of Lesbos)** – place name – an island in the E Aegean, off the NW coast of Turkey: a center of lyric poetry, led by Alcaeus and Sappho (6$^{th}$ century BCE); annexed to Greece in 1913

**Maimonides** – name – (1135-1204) called Moses

**Maimonides** (also known as Mūsā ibn Maymūn or **RaMBaM**, a Hebrew acronym for "**R**abbi **M**osheh **B**en **M**aimon"), preeminent medieval Jewish philosopher; one of the most prolific, followed *Torah* scholars and physicians of the Middle Ages

**Martial** – name – (40 CE - between 102 and 104 CE) Roman poet known for epigrams (1st century CE)

**Masturbation** – n. – sexual stimulation of one's own genitals, usually to point of orgasm

**Methodius** – name – Methodius of Olympus (died ca. 311); a Church Father and Saint who was a Christian bishop, ecclesiastical author, and martyr

*Mishnah* – Hebrew title – (pronounced MISH-nuh) the first written compilation of Jewish oral tradition (also called the *Oral Torah*), the basis of the *Talmud*, Includes Orders (chapters) and Tractates (verses)

**Mithras** – name – a Persian god from the Zoroastrian pantheon where he was a helper and assistant to the power of Good against the power of Evil

*Mitzvah* – Hebrew n. – (pronounced MITS-vuh) commandment; any of the 613 commandments that Jews are obligated to observe. It can also refer to any Jewish religious obligation, or more generally to any good deed.

*Mitzvah of Onah* – Hebrew n. – *Torah* ordained conjugal relations that are positively required of a married couple, separate and distinct from the need for procreation

*Mokh* – Hebrew n. – a birth-control device; literally means "to crush" or "to soften" and denotes a tuft of wool or cotton, or other absorbent device such as sea sponge; a medieval tampon

**Monasticism** – Greek n. – religious practice of renouncing worldly pursuits in order to devote oneself to spiritual work; monks and nuns are examples of *monastics*

**Mortal Sin** – phrase – In Roman Catholicism, a willful

violation of divine law in a serious matter; idolatry, adultery and murder, (sins against humanity) for example; Catholics carrying unconfessed mortal sins may not receive Communion.

**Narcissism** – n. – excessive self-love

**Neolithic** – n. – of or relating to the latest period of the Stone Age characterized by polished stone implements

***New Testament*** – title – the collection of the books of the *Bible* that were produced by the early Christian church, comprising the *Gospels, Acts of the Apostles,* the *Epistles,* and the *Revelation of St. John the Divine*; covenant between God and humans in which the dispensation of grace is revealed through Jesus Christ

**Nunnery** – n. – a place where nuns live

**Nymphomania** – n. – a neurotic condition in women; compulsion to have sexual intercourse with as many men as possible

***Olam Haba*** – Hebrew n. – (pronounced oh-LAHM hah-BAH) "the world to come" or the hereafter (heaven and hell for Christians). This concept is rarely discussed in Judaism

**Olisbos** – n. – object shaped like and used as substitute for erect penis; a dildo

**Olive oil method** – phrase – ancient method of birth control where olive oil is applied to the cervix; $4^{th}$ century CE Aristotle gave advice on how to prevent pregnancy, telling women to use olive oil, lead ointment, or frankincense oil as a spermicide

***Onah*** – Hebrew n. – mitzvah denoting sexual obligation of husband to wife

**Oral intercourse** – phrase – sexual contact between sex organs of one person and mouth of another; cunnilingus (performed on female) and felatio (performed on male)

**Orgasm** – n. – the sudden discharge of accumulated sexual tension during the sexual response cycle, resulti rhythmic muscular contractions in the pelvic region characterized by an intense sensation of pleasure

**Paleolithic** – adj. – of or relating to the cultural period of the Stone Age beginning with the earliest chipped stone tools, about 750,000 years ago, until the beginning of the Mesolithic Period, about 15,000 years ago

*Pasha* – Hebrew n. – (pronounced paw-shah') to breach; to transgress; used 136 times in biblical text, often mistakenly translated as "sin" in English Bible

*Pauline Epistles* – title – collection of letters written by the Apostle Paul of Tarsus; books in the *New Testament* that are traditionally attributed to Paul of Tarsus

**Pederasty** – n. – sexual relations of adult male with a prepubescent boy

**Pelvic cavity** – n. – body cavity bound by the bones of the pelvis

**Pelvic floor** – n. – pelvic diaphragm; composed of muscle fibers which span the area underneath the pelvis

**Penitence** – n. – sorrow for sins; remorse for wrongdoing

*Peritzut* – Hebrew n. – licentious behavior

**Peter Lombard** – name – (c. 1096-1164) a scholastic theologian and bishop and author of *Four Books of Sentences*, which became the standard textbook of theology, for which he earned the accolade *Magister Sententiarum*

**Platonic Dualism** – phrase – Plato's theory that the mind is identical with the soul, which both pre-existed and survived the body, going through a continual process of reincarnation or "transmigration;" the soul-body split in Plato

**lygamy** – n. – marriage in which a spouse of either sex may have more than one mate at the same time

**Gregory I** – name – (ca 540-604) also known as **·egory the Great**; pope from 590 until his death; known for his writings, which were more prolific than those of any of his predecessors as pope

**Pope Innocent III** – name – (1161-1216) one of the most powerful and influential popes of the Middle Ages

**Pope Siricius** – name – Bishop of Rome 384-399 CE; author of two decrees concerning clerical celibacy

**Presbyters** – n. – any elder of the congregation in the early Christian church

**Procreation** – n. – the act of conceiving offspring; reproduction

**Prurient** – adj. – unwholesome interest in sexual matters; lascivious

**Pubbococcogeal** – n. – muscle formed of fibers of the elevator muscle in the anus, arising from the pelvic surface of the body of the pubis, and attaching to the coccyx

**Pubic** – adj. – adjective for area of the human body near the pubes or the pubis; part of the body that forms the front of the pelvis

**Qadishtu** – Greek name – one of a class of sacred prostitutes found throughout the ancient Middle East, especially in worship of fertility goddess Astarte

**Rabbi Akiva** – Hebrew name – Akiva ben Joseph (ca.17-ca.137 CE) Rabbinic sage of the latter part of the 1$^{st}$ century and the beginning of the 2$^{nd}$ century; great authority of Jewish tradition and one of the most central and essential contributors to the *Mishnah* and *Midrash Halakha*; referred to in *Talmud* as "*Rosh la-Chachamim*" (Head of all the Sages); 7$^{th}$ most frequently mentioned sage in the *Mishnah*; considered by tradition to be one of the earliest founders of rabbinical Judaism

**Reformation** – proper n. – 16$^{th}$ century split within Western Christianity initiated by Martin Luther, John Calvin, and other early Protestants; their protests against the doctrines, rituals, and ecclesiastical structure of the Roman Catholic Church led to what we know today Protestant churches

**Romulus** – name – Roman myth; the founder of Rome, suckled with his twin brother Remus by a she-wolf after they were abandoned in infancy

**Saint Fulgentius** – name – (462-527) follower of St. Augustine's ideal of community life, a student of St. Augustine's theological teachings and a Bishop in the African Church in the city of Ruspe, North Africa

*Sandal* – Hebrew n. – fetus of a dual pregnancy; the fetuses when a woman becomes pregnant with a 2$^{nd}$ fetus when she is already pregnant

**Satyriasis** – n. – a neurotic condition in men; a compulsion to have sexual intercourse with as many women as possible; compared to nymphomania in women

**School of Hillel** – Hebrew phrase – founded by the famed Hillel the Elder, a school of Jewish law and thought that thrived in 1$^{st}$ century BCE Jerusalem; widely known for its hundreds of disputes with the School of Shammai; Most of the disputes between the two schools involve *halakha* (Jewish law); however, some involve arguments of Jewish philosophy

**School of Jesus** – Hebrew phrase – school of thought introduced by Jesus of Nazareth in 1$^{st}$ century Jerusalem and recorded today in the *Synoptic Gospels*

**School of Shammai** – Hebrew phrase – school of thought of Judaism founded by Shammai, a Jewish scholar of the 1$^{st}$ century; the most eminent contemporary and the *halachic* (Jewish law) opponent of the House of Hillel

***Shlom Bayyit*** – Hebrew phrase – lit "peace at home"; the Jewish religious concept of domestic harmony and good relations between husband and wife

**rapis** – name – a Greco-Egyptian god devised in the 3$^{rd}$ century BCE on the orders of Ptolemy I of Egypt to nify the Greeks and Egyptians in his realm

**l Continence** – phrase – self-restraint, especially ial

**Sex-role inversion** – phrase – complex situation in which one believes that he or she has been given the body of the wrong sex; emphasizes gender role reversal, resembles transgenderism

***Shaguf neheneh min haguf*** – Hebrew phrase – purpose of sexual relations for one body to find pleasure in the other

**Sodomy** – n. – anal intercourse with member of same or other sex; usually male on male

**Soranus of Ephesus** – name – (circa 98-138 CE) Greek physician from Ephesus; practiced in Alexandria and subsequently in Rome, a chief representative of the Methodic school of medicine; several of his writings still survive, most notably his four-volume treatise on gynecology, and a Latin translation of his: *On Acute and Chronic Diseases*

**Spermicide** – n. – an agent that kills spermatozoa, especially one used as a contraceptive

**Sphincter muscle** – phrase – any of the ring-like muscles surrounding, and able to contract or close a bodily passage or opening; i.e., sphincter pylori (that holds food in the stomach), the sphincter ani externus (holds anal opening closed), sphincter urethrae (controls urination), sphincter pupillae, (ring of fibres in the iris)

**Stoicism** – proper n. – ancient school of Greek philosophy, founded ca 300 BCE by Zeno; stressed wisdom as sole source of virtue, and virtue as evidenced mainly by indifference to the vicissitudes of fortune; Seneca (4 BCE-65 CE) and Marcus Aurelius (121-180 CE) are later followers

**Strato of Lampsacus** – name – (ca 335-270 BCE) Greek philosopher; denied supernatural forces at work in nature

**Syneisaktism** – n. –spiritual marriage; cohabitation by ascetics of different sexes without sexual relation; celibate marriage

**Talmud** – Hebrew title – (pronounced tahl'- mood) The *Gamara* (a commentary on the *Mishnah*) together with the *Mishnah* (the written oral law) is known as the *Talmud*. One compiled by Jewish scholars in Babylon (the *Babylonian Talmud*) and one compiled by Jewish scholars in the land of Israel (the *Jerusalem Talmud*). The *Babylonian Talmud* was completed ca 500 CE; the *Jerusalem Talmud* roughly a century earlier. It is a gigantic sea of rabbinic learning and the *Babylonian Talmud* is today the focus of Jewish religious education

**Talmudic Law** – Hebrew phrase – law derived from the *Talmud* based on the teachings of the Talmudic Sages

**Tertullian** – name – **Quintus Septimius Florens Tertullianus**, (c. 160-c. 225 CE), a prolific early Christian author from Carthage in the Roman province of Africa. He is the first Christian author to produce an extensive corpus of Latin Christian literature

**Torah** – Hebrew title – (Pronounced toh'-rah) the entire body of Jewish religious literature, law, and teaching as contained chiefly in the Old Testament and the Talmud; the Pentateuch (first five books of Old Testament), being the first of the three Jewish divisions of the Old Testament

**Tours** – place name – City in west central France on river Loire; site of various Roman Catholic Church councils in Middle Ages, the first in 461

**Transsexual** – n. – a person whose sexual identification is entirely with the opposite sex

**Tribad** – n. – female, usually homosexual, with large clitoris (sometimes spelled "tribade")

**ginal orgasm** – phrase – orgasm in female derived from vaginal penetration or a blend of clitoral and -Spot stimulation; also referred to as G-Spot orgasm

**Sin** – phrase – in Roman Catholicism, a lesser and rgivable sin

**Vicissitude** – n. – recurrent changes; ups and downs

***YHWH*** – name – a tetragrammaton for four Hebrew letters (*Yod*, *He*, *Waw* and *He*) the name of the Almighty Father in Heaven that people commonly call "The LORD" or "God"

**Zeno of Citium** – name – (The Stoic) (333 BCE-264 BCE) Hellenistic philosopher of Phoenician origin from Citium, Cyprus; founder of Stoic school of philosophy named for his teaching platform, the Painted Porch ("stoa" is Greek for "porch")

***Zenut*** – Hebrew n. – unlawful sexual behavior, especially prostitution

**Zoophilia** – n. – sexual attraction to animals, a.k.a. bestiality

# ABOUT THE AUTHOR

Dr. Roy B. Blizzard is President of Bible Scholars, Inc., an Austin-based corporation dedicated to biblical research and education. A native of Joplin, Missouri, he attended Oklahoma Military Academy and has a B.A. degree from Phillips University in Enid, Oklahoma. He has an M.A. degree from Eastern New Mexico University in Portales, New Mexico, an M.A. degree from the University of Texas at Austin, and a Ph.D. in Hebrew Studies from the University of Texas at Austin. From 1968 to June 1974, he was an instructor in Hebrew, Biblical History and Biblical Archaeology at the University of Texas at Austin. Dr. Blizzard is today a professor at the American Institute for Advanced Biblical Studies in Little Rock, Arkansas.

Dr. Blizzard has spent much of his time in Israel and the Middle East in study and research. He has hosted over 500 television programs about Israel and Judaism for various television networks and is a frequent television and radio guest. He is the author of numerous books and articles which can be found listed on the Bible Scholars Website, in the bookstore.

Dr. Blizzard is nationally certified as an educator in Marriage and Family relationships and human sexuality. He is a Diplomate with the American Board of Sexology and continues to conduct a private practice in the field of sex education and therapy.

OTHER BOOKS BY ROY B. BLIZZARD

*Mishnah and the Words of Jesus*

*Tithing Giving and Prosperity*

*The Mountain of the Lord*

*Let Judah Go Up First: A Study in Praise, Prayer, and Worship*

David Bivin and Roy Blizzard, Jr., *Understanding the Difficult Words of Jesus: New Insights From a Hebrew Perspective*

Visit us online at
www.thebiblesexandyou.com

Bible Scholars, Inc.
P. O. Box 204073
Austin, Texas 78720

www.biblescholars.org

*Dedicated to supporting, developing and promoting future Bible Scholars.*

Made in the USA
Middletown, DE
06 March 2024

50931688R00092